AF342582

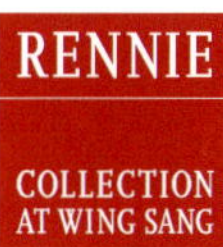

RENNIE
COLLECTION
AT WING SANG

2 March to 8 June 2013

ROBERT BECK
ROBERT BUCK

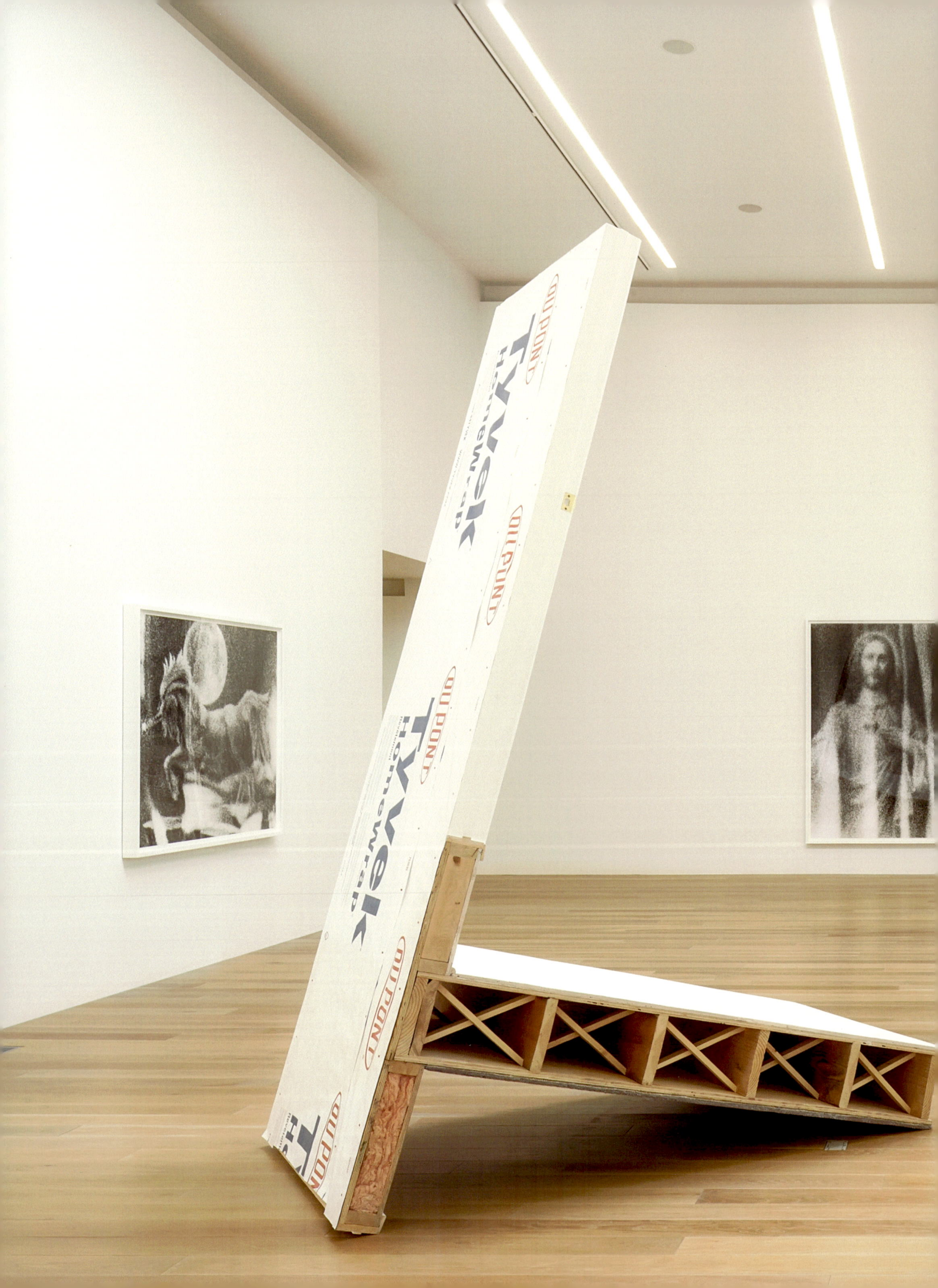

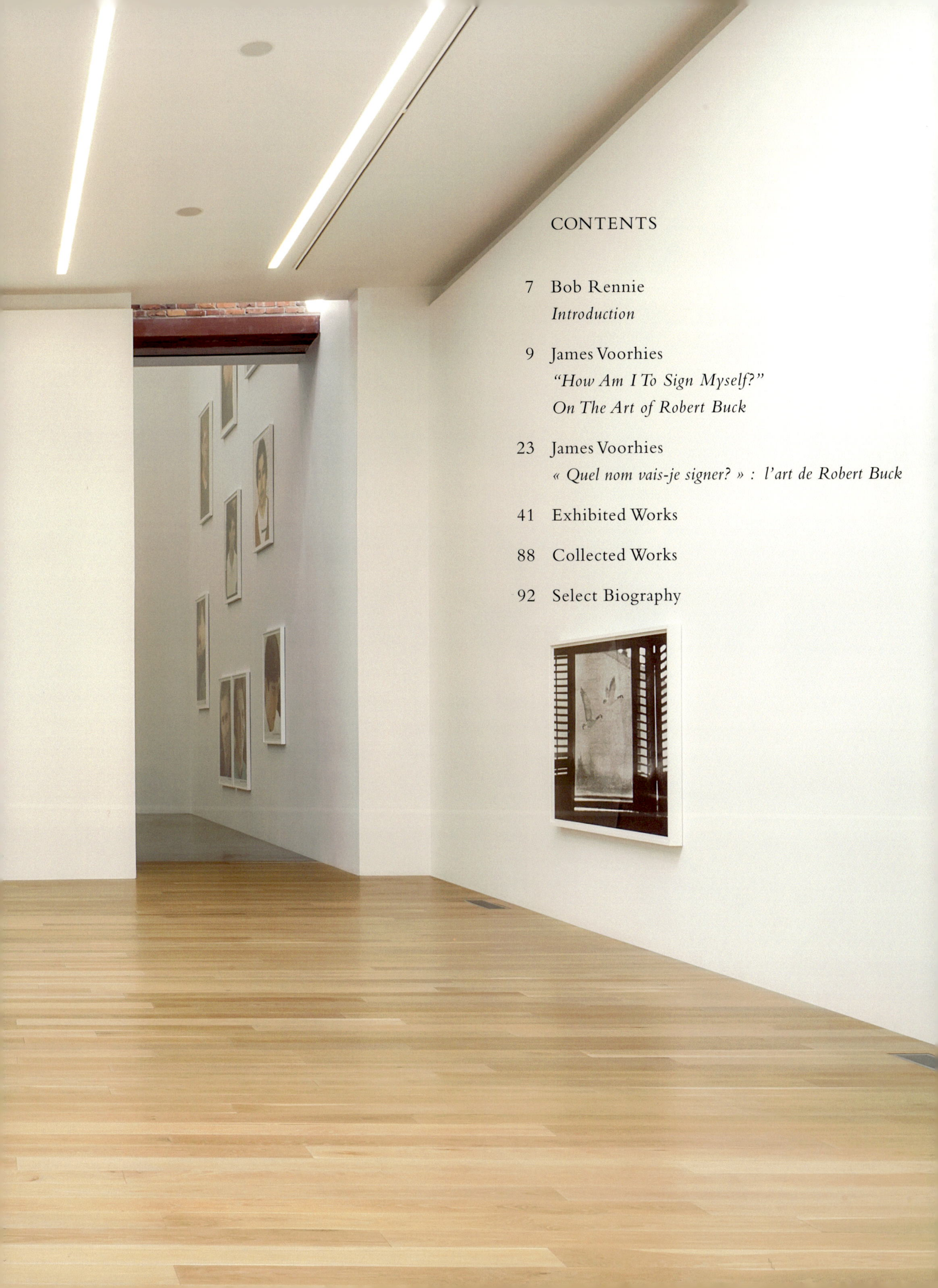

CONTENTS

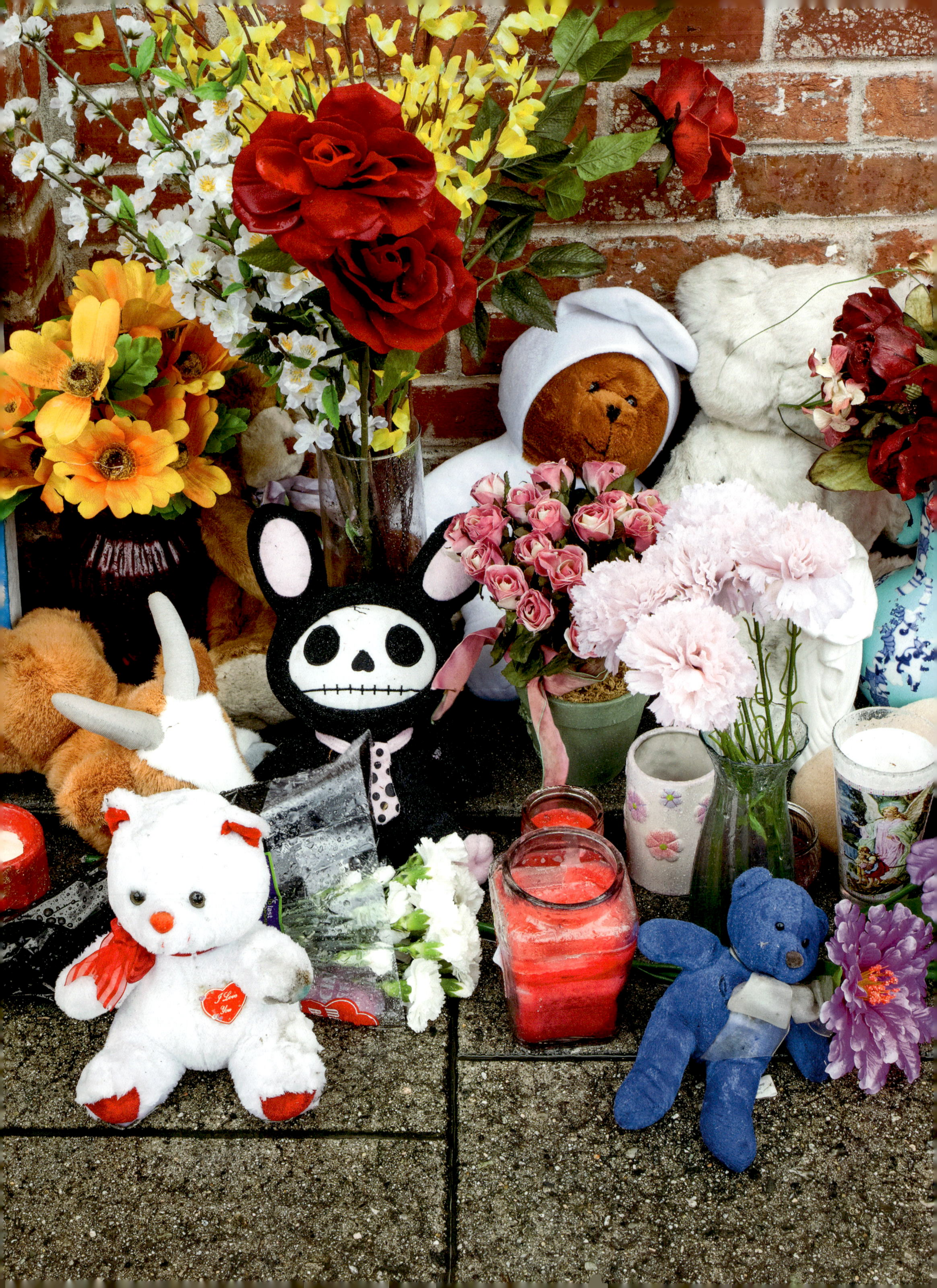

ROBERT BECK / ROBERT BUCK

Bob Rennie

How do I sign myself? This is a conversation that Bob (Robert Beck formerly and currently Robert Buck) and I—collector, friend and custodian of an artist's journey—have appropriately had many, many times.

One of the *Thirteen Shooters* photographs was my introduction to Bob Beck's oeuvre and I subsequently acquired the full set. The discussion surrounding this body of work touched on how mistakenly proud I would have been if one of the deceptively innocent-looking boys depicted were to date my daughter. Yet, those boys were not innocent. They were killers. What went wrong to result in children who murder? *Screen Memory (Mother's Room, Father's Room, Brother's Room, Sister's Room and Family Room)* along with *Wall Ceiling ("Bless This House…")* just might hint at the "cause" of such violence. This and other continuing dialogues lead to the constant exploration, not only of the content of Bob's work, but of the process of collecting an artist's work in depth and the responsibilities of being the custodian of an artist's career.

Think about it. Each room in your childhood home holds deeply felt positive moments and penetratingly negative moments. Which of these memories do you highlight? Which memories do you erase? This is where Bob takes us. I liken the *Screen Memory* photographs to hearing a song on the radio that stirs one's emotions—a tear is formed or a smile bursts out from the experience and memories. The same experience occurs as you look through this catalogue; the evidence of an extraordinary practice emerges. A practice that demands more of the viewer than it provides answers, and that is Art.

Carey Fouks, my family and I are very proud of our journey with Robert Buck. His practice talks to our collection in the same way that the work of Mona Hatoum, Kerry James Marshall, Christian Boltanski and Larry Clark's *Tulsa* does. All of these artists address the question of what makes the human spirit. Be it positive or negative, that spirit simply exists.

Now, how do I sign myself? I will sign myself as I have always done in my emails to Bob… "love, Bob."

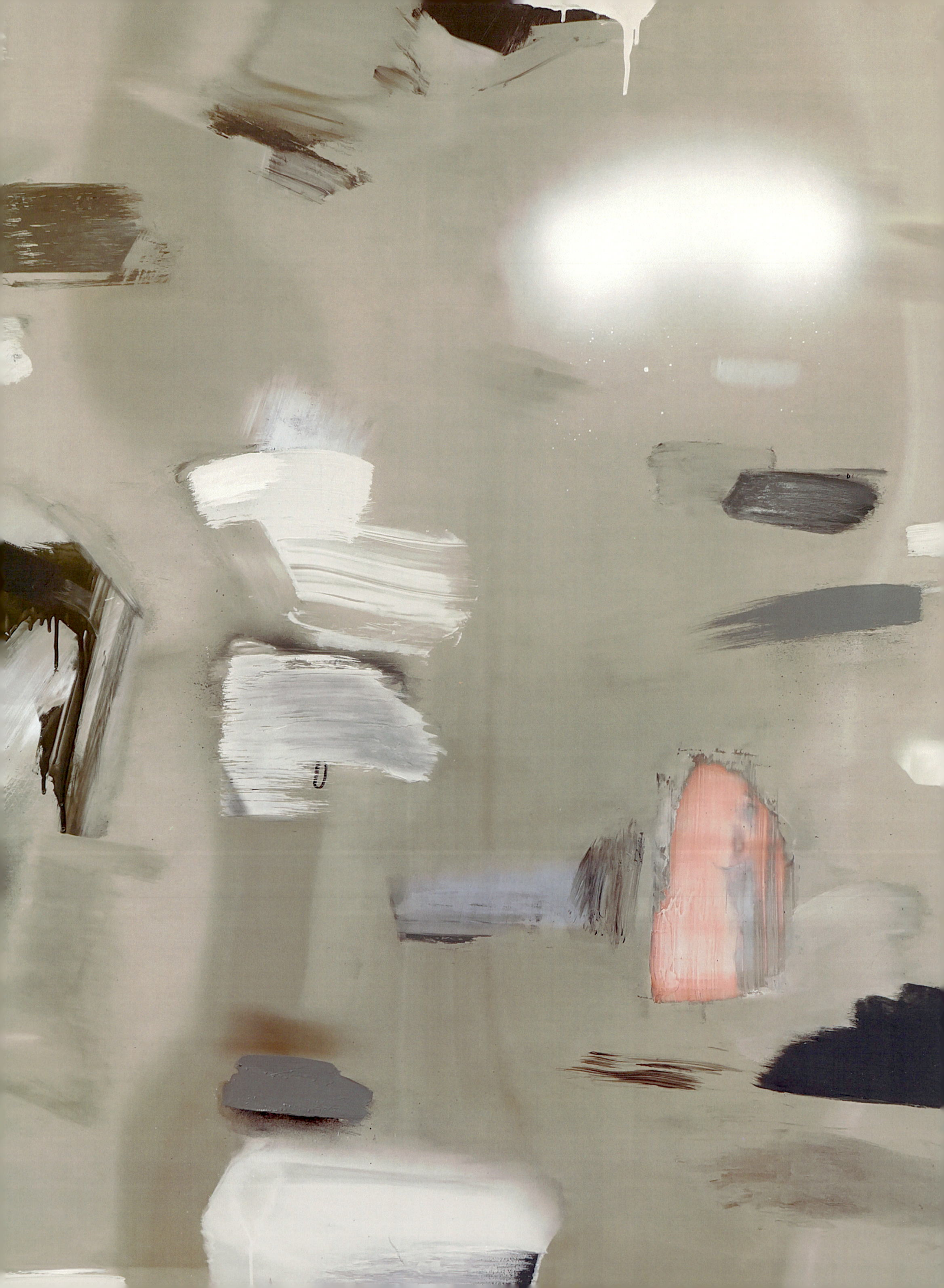

"HOW AM I TO SIGN MYSELF?"
ON THE ART OF ROBERT BUCK

James Voorhies

On a sidewalk near the entrance to a gallery on East Pender Street in Vancouver, British Columbia, visitors to Robert Buck's exhibition encounter a makeshift shrine. A motley collection of stuffed animals, scented candles, framed photographs and poems sit alongside fresh carnations, dahlias and lilies. Some flowers are airbrushed bright fuchsia or purple. Others are plastic. Cellophane balloons, a plastic angel and a ceramic flowerpot in the shape of a wide-eyed doe are among the disparate objects. Public displays of grief like this appear in response to untimely deaths, sometimes connected to the site of a bicycle or car accident. Other times they signify the collective mourning of a widely known loss of life, such as a mass shooting at an elementary school or a suburban Cineplex. These kinds of memorials were common sites in the weeks following the massacre that killed twenty first-graders and six adults at Sandy Hook Elementary School in Newtown, Connecticut, in 2012. Viewers of news reports on television and digital screens witnessed images of communal shrines springing up in sympathy around the globe. The images were visual accompaniment to audio reports that attempted to relay, or even humanize, the events. This shrine in Vancouver, in front of this gallery at this moment, while cause for pause and reflection, is, unfortunately, not out of the ordinary given the culture of increasingly widespread violence.

When entering Robert Buck's exhibition at the Rennie Collection, periodic but distinctive sounds of gunshots greet visitors. Their source is not obvious, out of sight and coming from somewhere at the rear of the gallery. But the sounds contribute to an unease already initiated by the shrine outside. The work *Untitled (Daly Over/Under @ Close Range w/.12 "Punkin' Ball" Slug) (Entrance and Exit)* (1999) hangs to the right of the entrance. It is a diptych with two spiral-bound drawing pads. A hole made with a "punkin' ball" slug pierces the centre of each surface. The hole produced by a shot entering from the front is roughly an inch in diameter with gradations of blacks and greys radiating from its dark core. Delicately variegated marks appear as though drawn by chance with mushroom spores or flower pollen. The pad shot from the reverse is forced outward like a budding blossom. Violent acts made these marks. But the surfaces are left paradoxically beautiful.

Robert Beck
Untitled (Clean), 2004
mixed media on stainless steel
57 ¾ x 65 ¾ x ¾ inches
(146.7 x 167 x 1.9 cm)

Hanging on the wall opposite, *A part from the Whole (Communion)* (2005) is eleven photographs united in the form of an oversized composite frame, the cheap kind used to gather together snapshots from proms, weddings or family picnics. The images are cropped photos from the First Holy Communions of a Catholic boy and girl, including close-ups of hands clasped in prayer or holding a songbook. References to both father and mother are present in a few images. In one photo, the shadow of the father screens across the son's body, making its mark at the precise moment the image is taken. In another, the father's right hand rests on the son's shoulder while, in another, the mother is seen holding sunglasses. This underlying visual terrain emerges from the larger pictures of childhood events (to which we are not privy) visible through squares, rectangles and a single, circular frame where the praying hands of the boy are pictured. This circular opening recalls the classical tondo of Renaissance painting, a form traditionally reserved for religious portrayals of mother and child. While these symbolic rituals of purification are portrayed in *Communion*, physical attempts to cleanse are etched into the surface of *Untitled (Clean)* (2004), which hangs nearby. This shiny steel bathroom partition bolted flush to the wall implicates spectators as they enter the exhibition. Removed from its original function of dividing public toilets and guiding social behaviour, spectators catch their hazy, fleeting images in the reflective surface, cast among various scratches and patches of colour.

As the sounds of gunshots continue to resonate throughout the gallery, spectators are lured further into it. The life-size drawing *Two-Pin Toggle ("The Modern Man's Guide to Life" by Denise Boyles, Alan Rose, Alan Wellikoff)* (2001) hangs at the end of a corridor. Using charcoal on one large sheet of paper, the artist reproduces an illustration from the book *The Modern Man's Guide to Life* (1987) that instructs readers (presumably adolescent males) on how to be a man. This drawing is an enlarged version of an illustration of how to capture small animals. The two-pin toggle is a trapping technique where small, notched pieces of wood are looped with string and placed into the ground to make a snare. *Two-Pin Toggle* shows us how masculinity is deeply inscribed at an early age through a discourse buttressed in images and language.

Turning attention away from the drawing, spectators discover the video *Untitled (Dec. 29, 1993)* (1999) installed in a dimly lighted corner behind the stairwell. A television monitor sits on an audio/visual cart, positioned precisely at the level of a viewer's eyes. Small speakers sit on the shelf below. And, here it is, the origin of those sounds of the discharging rifle. They emanate from this anthropomorphic audio-visual installation where spectators stand before the video, looking directly into a black-and-white screen of throbbing white concentric circles that recall the constricting and relaxing muscles of a pupil or sphincter. Stamped with the date and time, "Dec. 29, 1993," the video is a result of a fully-functioning, automatic lens that continually recalibrates in search of its subject, a subject forever fleeting because the cap remains on the lens. Spectators eagerly watch and wait for a representational image to fulfil our increasingly desperate reliance on the visual for understanding anything. Spectators contend, however, with the mesmerizing, target-like circles of libidinal energy while they listen, ever so carefully, to the muffled voices of two men intermixed with low rumbles caused by wind tickling the microphone. We hear the anxious, impatient voice of a father instructing a son on how to shoot a gun while the son, in turn, gives lessons to the father on how to operate a camera. Their brief exchanges include debates over how to hold the gun, if it is in a locked position and some confusion about whether or not the camera is on. Their words are interspersed with an uncomfortable silence interrupted by that sound heard since walking into the exhibition: a gunshot—louder and more intense now.

I. [*I always speak the truth*]

These works of art were conceived and produced by Robert Beck before the self-nomination, in 2008, from Beck to Buck. His practice defies categorization and thwarts the usual mechanisms for identifying an artist through a particular style, medium and even a name. His sculptures, drawings, paintings, texts, videos, installations and exhibitions appropriate familiar forms—like a makeshift shrine and an illustration from a "how to" manual. The artist draws on the belief associated with those forms in order to disrupt expectations of them. Spontaneous public memorials, for instance, are accompanied by the basic understanding that someone died. And, in turn, someone cared enough to mark that event and subsequently other people cared enough to buy, make or leave a memento in remembrance of it. Part of the experience of a sidewalk shrine assumes all this is true. *The Shrine (from e to u)* (2000/2012), which spectators encountered before entering the gallery, promises the appearance of such. It demands the same as any other sidewalk shrine; to be experienced as a response to a tragic event. However, when spectators realize it is not specific to an actual event, such as Sandy Hook, the form speaks a partial truth of what we come to expect from it. The appropriation eclipses assumptions embedded in these kinds of familiar forms and as artworks they become openings with potential for revealing broader political and social implications connected to their existence in the first place.

The political in the art of Robert Buck, however, is not an obvious critique of, say, gun control. Buck's art does not seek to make specific judgements on these conditions. We don't learn his position on guns and, in fact, need to question if that knowledge is important for responding to the work. By reframing and recontextualizing the familiar, the political in his art surfaces in ways that utilize the spectator's experience of reality, their understanding of the way things are, and juxtaposes it within a topology that charts a physical and mental course of reading the exhibition by moving and thinking through it, even if it reaches out of the gallery onto the sidewalk. Buck arranges the exhibition as a topology to draw together inherently partial truths that individual works speak. *The Shrine* has no more political bearing than any other makeshift memorial, unless it is inserted into the realm of art and understood amongst other works in an exhibition, such as the video *Dec. 29, 1993*, the photograph *Communion* and the drawing *Two-Pin Toggle*. When these works are encountered in the context of one another, they read like a text where each signifier-cum-artwork becomes part of a sentence exploring the sweeping structural effects societal institutions, such as family, race, sexuality, religion, media, education and language, have on politics and culture—the way we live now. This combination of familiarity and confusion leverages that sweet space of a politics of aesthetics by altering the appearance of things, repositioning our perspectives. And that is where the critical rests. That is what has the potential to change perceptions and generate new meaning and understanding of the world. When visitors exit the gallery they read *The Shrine* differently than when they entered.

I always speak the truth. Not the whole truth,
because there's no way, to say it all. Saying it all is
literally impossible: words fail. Yet it's through this
very impossibility that the truth holds onto the real.

These words are part of a televised interview with the French psychoanalyst, Jacques Lacan. In January 1973, the young academic and analyst-in-training, Jacques-Alain Miller, asked Lacan to do the interview because he "wanted Lacan, just once, to speak to the common man."[1] Originally broadcast under the title "Psychoanalysis" on a French government TV network, the two-part program was simultaneously published as a book titled *Television*, which is the organizing framework for this text on the art of Robert Buck.[2] *Television* is divided into seven sections and, like the televised program, full of playful responses, cryptic comments, serious ruminations and incongruent statements by Lacan that reflect the "comedy," as he says, of summarizing psychoanalysis. Indeed, his quizzical and surprising appearance on screen—tinged with satire— signals an awareness of the impossible, even ridiculous, task of talking generally about the private practice of psychoanalysis for public consumption. Throughout the interview, however, he does 13 exactly what was asked of him; he performs the psychoanalyst figure.

Psychoanalytic theory by Jacques Lacan is reconstituted out of Freud. But unlike Freud, for Lacan consciousness becomes irrelevant to psychoanalysis. Psychoanalysis, according to early Lacan, is a means for reading, witnessing and coming to terms with the unconscious—as it is. Lacan's fundamental axiom is that the unconscious is structured like a language. That, however, is something of a paradox: language is also what allows a reading of the unconscious and thus a discourse of psychoanalysis to even exist. So while the unconscious can never be fully elucidated or reconciled, it can be apprehended through its traces—slips of the tongue, jokes, bungled actions, dreams. Instances of the unconscious that surface in reality are half-truths with the structure of fiction that take shape and significance through a shared dialogue between an analyst and a subject. This exchange is based on language that manifests through free association, through what the speaking-being has to say. Analysis, therefore, is a critical reflection of the discourse, or social links, where the human subject has no choice but to speak, as manifested through the traces of the unconscious, which ciphers and processes each moment of every single day. Lacan's broadcast on television promised a position of teaching about psychoanalysis. But it partook in a refusal of that promise because his appearance was in actuality a performance of failure. And, that failure reflected the logical impossibility to adequately communicate an understanding of the unconscious and define psychoanalysis.

For there's no difference between television and the
public before whom I've spoken for a long time now,
a public known as my seminar. A single gaze in both
cases: a gaze to which, in neither case, do I address
myself, but in the name of which I speak.

II. [The unconscious, a very precise thing]

In Buck's exhibition spectators ascend the stairs to a second-floor gallery. Here, they enter an enormous space with soaring 11.8 metre ceilings where the photographic series *Thirteen Shooters* (2001) is installed from floor to ceiling opposite the entrance.[3] The large 17.8 by 9 metre gallery combined with towering ceilings reflects a basilica-like architecture, accentuated by the apsidal backdrop of pictures of young men. Thirteen movie-poster-size inkjet prints of individual portraits of teenage boys utilize appropriated photographic imagery and text. Our attention is drawn immediately inward and upward toward this altar/shrine where the casual arrangement compares to images cascading from the sky or scrolling down a laptop screen on Tumblr. The portraits command an extraordinary visual power over the experience of the entire space. The pictures are colour and Ben-Day dots, cropped from various newspapers; some are more formal yearbook photos or personal snapshots drawn from photos taken at sporting events and family gatherings. Others are decidedly journalistic, taken at hearings or when exiting a courthouse. Beck provides captions for each image. But the words do not reveal the given or paternal names of the boys. Instead they are names of media sources and photographers: "Reuters," "Corbis Sygma," "Associated Press," "Elaine Thomas—AP" and "San Diego Union-Tribune." Front and centre and confronting the spectator's gaze head on is a diptych of Eric Harris and Dylan Klebold; the same iconic photos that emblazoned television screens in the late 1990s, following Columbine and today permanently archived on Wikipedia. In this installation these portraits act as centrifugal forces toward which the other photographs of young shooters gravitate.

Although *Thirteen Shooters* has a different boy pictured in each of the photographs, the range and variability of portrait types represent the singular identity construed by the media of the iconic teenage shooter. In other words, just hours after a mass shooting, photographs of the perpetrator from kindergarten, grade school, soccer matches and high-school proms are invariably rounded up for public consumption. The ensuing days find more photos from an arraignment and sentencing. The media edits and formulates a composite identity of a shooter by circulating these kinds of images with speed and acuity.

While Beck withholds names of the boys pictured in *Thirteen Shooters*, the sculpture *Artwork by Kip Kinkel for His Parents Bill and Faith* (2004), in the same gallery includes real names in his exploration of the combined effects of family and media on the formation of identity. In Oregon in 1998, Kinkel's shooting rampage took the lives of his mother and father and two high-school classmates. *Artwork* combines the ubiquitous forms of "welcome" and "bath" mats; each cast and presented in a way that resembles headstones. These sculptures are moulded out of white silicone. Seven bullets cast of wound filler, a waxy substance used to fill the holes in bodies as they are prepared for public viewings at funerals, are scattered across the surfaces. The number of bullets equals that used by Kinkel to kill his parents, six for his mother and one for his father.

Hanging nearby, text and image also intersect in a series of "diagnostic" drawings by Beck. The drawings are based on published sources of a variety of different psychological tests used to assess a subject's personality. One test is called the House-Tree-Person (HTP) personality-assessment technique. The psychologist John N. Buck developed it in the 1960s. Subjects are asked to draw the above-mentioned objects and then respond to an extensive list of questions about what they drew. A qualitative evaluation of the patient is based on subjective interpretation of their responses and images. These works by Beck are a combination of actual drawings by patients and comments by their analysts, all rendered by the artist in his own hand. Beck uses latent fingerprint powder, the same dusting agent that police use at crime scenes, to fill in various background areas and make fingerprint smudges.

Also included in this gallery is the sculpture *01/25/04–Shots No. 12, 13, 14 (Daly Over/Under at Close Range with .12 Gauge "Punkin' Ball" Slug)* (2004). It is made with three plastic, 25-gallon buckets, rammed full of flesh-coloured wound filler. Comparable to the drawing *Entrance and Exit*, Beck discharged at close range a single shot in each bucket; this time deep into the fat-like substance leaving a cavernous hole in the material bulging up and over the circular rims. The very substance used to repair wounds, here adopts a corporeal quality, punctured but in fact irreparable. Opposite *Thirteen Shooters* is *'ccused of K (The New York Times, Nov 30, 2002)* (2003), a 2.6 by 2.1 metre reproduction of a doe-eyed teenage boy with beautiful curly locks looking forlornly and directly at the spectator. The image was appropriated from a newspaper article about the two King brothers—Alex and Derek—who in 2001 were accused and convicted of killing their father as he slept in a La-Z-boy. Beck has meticulously reproduced, by hand, a section of the article. These works speak to a culture of celebrity worship not limited to movie stars, teen idols and sports icons, and where the lessons of masculinity explored in *Two-Pin Toggle* and *Dec. 29, 1993* go completely awry.

He thinks as a consequence of the fact that a structure, that of language—the word implies it—a structure carves up his body, a structure that has nothing to do with anatomy.

Language structures our reality. For Lacan, the unconscious is a precise thing because it manifests within the contingencies imposed upon us by language. Through speech and because of speech, we cannot fully realize desire and something always remains of it in the unconscious. This immersion in language is both a permissible and prohibitive factor in our negotiations between everyday life and the unconscious because language is never able to completely convey what we want it to say and do. Within a consideration of the function of language, Lacan's theory of the symbolic order is often called the "Name-of-the-Father." According to this theory, which is based on a reformulation of Freud's Oedipal complex, societal law is determined—literally and metaphorically—by the name of the father. Our name comes from this paternal law, which is the very foundation upon which we learn to name and understand the world. It is the first experience we have with language, and that initial encounter is determined by the circumstances of family, the desire for the mother, the "no" of the father. For Lacan, it is through the paternal function of language that social behaviour is ordered. However, he later reworked the paternal law as the "Names-of-the-Father," pluralizing it to reflect its singular function for every single one of us. Self-nomination holds the potential to create new links beyond these governing forces of family. The new constellations reconfigure the subject's existence in language, opening up new possibilities for its binding effects to become undone, reconstituted through the symbolic act of re-naming. As an invention, that act is a reclamation and reorientation of desire.

III. [*Being a saint*]

One thing is certain: to take the misery onto one's
shoulders is to enter into the discourse that
determines it, even if only to protest.

In the gallery adjacent to where *Thirteen Shooters* is installed, the order of the family is a predominant theme. Installed in the centre of this space is the sculpture *Wall Ceiling ("Bless This House…")* (2004). The work is a cross-section from a larger architectural whole. An insulated wall, inverted, stands upright with the ceiling positioned at a right angle to the wall, appearing as though excised with utmost precision. The modest, even cheap, quality of this wall and ceiling is comparable to ubiquitous American vernacular, suburban "rec" rooms. Beck's recontextualization of this anywhere, anyplace architecture is a playful challenge to the values associated with American family identity and the physical and symbolic stability invested in it. A framed poem hangs upside down on the wall: "Bless this house/Oh Lord we pray/Make it safe/By night and day."

Five large-scale, grainy photographs are installed on the perimeter of this gallery and radiate with watchful intensity around *Wall Ceiling* and the spectators. These large-scale, black-and-white silver gelatin prints are titled *Screen Memory* (2004) with parenthetical titles *Father's Room, Mother's Room, Brother's Room, Sister's Room* and *Family Room.* The series' title refers to Freud's theory of memories from childhood where seemingly insignificant details are stand-ins or screens for more significant childhood experiences and events. Each photograph is characterized by simultaneous reflections of different domestic spaces that become overall surrogate portraits of family members. *Mother's Room*, for example, has an iconic image of Jesus Christ looking piously downward with dark curtains partially pulled open and reflected in the glass of the dime-store reproduction. *Father's Room* is an image with a picture of a pair of geese soaring into the air while shutters and the afternoon sun filtering into a dusty room are revealed in its reflection. Although *Mother's Room* hangs in close proximity to *Father's Room*, they are installed on completely separate walls. *Brother's Room* has an eagle and American flag; *Sister's Room* includes a prominent image of a unicorn. The artist's room, however, is conspicuously absent.

At this point I will interject a remark. I do not base
this idea of discourse on the ex-sistence of the
unconscious. It is the unconscious that I locate
through it—it ex-sists only through a discourse.

IV. [*These faint gestures by which one tries to shield against my discourse*]

Beck's *dust (Community Times, June 20, 1965)* (1998/2006) consumes a 17.8-metre–long, 1.4-metre–wide passageway dividing two galleries. In this immersive, restrictive environment a 13-metre wall is painted floor to ceiling with dark, slate paint to create a chalkboard surface. Written by hand, with white chalk across the surface of the entire wall, are texts—articles, advertisements, obituaries and classifieds—from an edition of the *Community Times*, which was the artist's hometown weekly, dated June 20, 1965. Most of the words are erased leaving a hazy filter through which the spectator's eyes wander across the surface, while physically moving through the space of the corridor and trying to make sense of the partially effaced texts. Beck's symbolic and real assault on how we know and exist in the world draws upon and unites experiences with education and media. Added to the conflation of classroom and newsprint here, a small, framed Polaroid photograph hangs on one wall. The snapshot signifies literal death in the image of a child's tombstone that lures spectators down the passageway where religion, education, memory and media collide in a singular immersive moment.

dust is simultaneously construction and defacement of language; a physical gesture against screens of interpretation and editing that guide and define our understanding of the world from adolescence to adulthood. And, we stand here before this towering wall of language where the partially erased text reflects a truth understood by what is present as much as absent in overlapping modes of remembering and forgetting.

Affect, therefore, befalls a body whose essence it is
said is to dwell in language—I am borrowing plumage
which sells better than my own—affect, I repeat,
befalls it on account of its not finding dwelling-
room, at least not to its taste.

V. [*This knowledge in as much as it does not think*]

The evidence of erasure is permanently etched into the surface of *Wall Hung Urinal Screen ("Big Red")* (2003), a bathroom partition, like *Untitled (Clean),* removed from a place of dividing spaces and male bodies in public-toilet stalls. Here, in the gallery the partition becomes an abstract painting and sculpture hanging perpendicular to the wall, which spectators must negotiate in a different manner. The precision with which the artist has replicated the form generates an uncertainty as to its place as art or artefact. Its off-white enamel paint is marked with phrases such as "Jerk Off," "MOTHERFUCKINGMINT," SEX ME MOMMY" and "BIG RED." The latter scratched next to a rudimentary drawing of a gigantic penis. The words are visible within the context of *Mother's Room* and *Father's Room* in the adjacent gallery and from opposite perspectives. These transgressive acts are common sights in high-school bathrooms where boys engage in recurring performances with school officials over use of walls for disseminating uninhibited speech. Produced anonymously, texts and images in public bathrooms—however temporary— symbolize the release of latent desire without the usual burdens of societal censure.

There lies a chance for us to be in touch with the real pure and simple—as
that which prevents one from saying the whole *truth about it.*

Hidden Pictures (At Rest) (2004) is also in this gallery. It is a 1.2 by 2.8 metre graphite drawing on paper based on the "Hidden Pictures" page of the American children's magazine *Highlights*. Functioning on a less formal diagnostic level than the House-Tree-Person personality tests, the monthly journal started in the 1940s using crafts, jokes, puzzles and games to educate children who search between the lines of a drawing to find random objects such as a ballpoint pen or fish defined by contours of bigger scenes such as a farmyard or vegetable market. *Hidden Pictures (At*

Rest) is based on a page called "Corn City," a fantasy city fashioned out of corn cobs. The caption instructs children to look for a snowman, palm tree, candle, scarf, campfire and a boy, among other images. Beck erased everything but one image in the larger illustration. It is a child's body resting horizontal in the furrows of a road, as if disinterred. Hardly the "boy" one might expect to find in a playful children's game. To the right of the overall scene are several feet of blank paper, an empty space—a void—inviting futile attempts at seeing something that helps clarify this uncertain scenario. While the diagnostic drawings sought meaning in the texts and images, there is nothing here to explain this unsettling scene, which is extracted—or highlighted—from the larger picture of things.

Who doesn't know that it's with the analytic
discourse that I've made it big. That makes me a
self-made man.

VI. [Knowing, doing, hoping]

In 1974, Lacan performed a refusal of identity on television. His presence on the screen promised to define psychoanalysis. But, in essence, he withheld a quick-and-easy explication from the mass-viewing public by refusing to reduce a complex body of ideas and knowledge to a single explanation. In 2008, the artist Robert Beck changed his name to Robert Buck. Artists too perform different expected functions in order to satisfy different constituents that include dealers, collectors, museums, art fairs, academia and critics. These constituents form the "institution of art" that projects demands onto the artist figure. The artist figure is human capital. And human capital is raised and maintained through a continual public performance of identity, which includes lecturing, exhibiting, writing, travelling, socializing and teaching. These performances contribute to the overall perception of the artist, helping him to retain economic and cultural value, remain relevant and legitimize himself as the artist figure.

Artists participate in a performance of this discourse. For a mid-career artist such as Beck there was already considerable infrastructure built around that identity—the brand "Robert Beck"—and the assumption of its ongoing performance. The transformation from the artist Robert Beck to the artist Robert Buck was a provocation to this discourse, disturbing and decentralizing the institution of art that attempts to thwart that kind of challenge through its ongoing perpetuation of singularity, of subjectivity, invested in the belief of a name as identity—embodied in the signature of the artist.

The extraordinary attention to building and maintaining individual identity is not limited to the realm of art. The early to mid-2000s left us with an unprecedented emphasis on the marketing of individual identity and the personalization of digital personas. The corporate names (let alone functions) of Myspace, YouTube and Facebook signal the placement of the individual above all else.[4] In our current predicament, emails and social-network posts are trolled and then analyzed in algorithms that supply and placate us with consumer choices we have actually told information capital we want. Technology constantly tailors and refines our buying habits through the words we write in Gmail, the things we buy on Amazon, watch on Netflix and hear on iTunes. One need also consider the number of artists whose last names are followed by the suffix ".com" in website and email addresses that inherently assign a commercial value to the identity of the artist. In an era of relentless attention to identity, especially the individual consumer of all things—education, fashion, information, image and health—we fall prey to the singularities assigned to us.

The artist develops out of these complicated circumstances of history and commerce that are reinforced by the institution of art. Capital is an organism inextricably linked to human desire. Contemporary society is fuelled by systems of production and consumption where capital exploits our desires in order to move itself forward, just as Freud theorized the pleasure principle is the underlying libidinal pulse of our every decision and action. The artist figure is required to step before the public in various ways to communicate with and touch the consumer. Through formations of erasure, editing and partial truths, the self-nomination of Robert Buck challenges conditions related to the identity of the artist figure, casting shadows over governing structures in art and language that define being artist.

Must I repeat that it is only in relation to a
discourse that such a subject can be truly located,
namely in relation to something whose artificiality
concretizes it.

VII. [*What is well-spoken, one conceives it clearly*]

"How am I to sign myself?" writes James Joyce to his lover Nora Barnacle in the close of a letter from 1904. The uncertainty associated with this simple question reveals a knowing awareness of the limits of language and its power over the determination of identity. Ostensibly the same question prevails throughout this exhibition by Robert Buck where works gathered together explore various processes of identity, from the diagnostic drawings, *Thirteen Shooters* and *dust* to *Hidden Pictures*, the *Screen Memory* photographs and the lithographic series *How Am I to Sign Myself* (2008), the title of which departs from Joyce's quixotic inquiry. Buck's *How Am I to Sign Myself* is a print in twenty-four parts that includes the names of visitors to the 2007 exhibition of the same title at CRG Gallery in New York City; his last exhibition as Robert Beck. Utilizing the readymade form of his dealer's letterhead and the ubiquitous guestbook, Buck appropriates the names of visitors, drawing attention to the periodic practice of presenting a body of work to a mass-viewing public. *How Am I to Sign Myself*, the first work to follow the self-nomination from Beck to Buck, shows the stream of exhibition goers identified by their signature. Unlike the absence in his series of *Screen Memory* photographs, the artist is absolutely present here with the signature "R. Buck." Just as Joyce's letter to his lover finally closed with the statement "I won't sign anything at all, because I don't know what to sign myself," Robert Buck's self-nomination with the simple change "from e to u" stakes a claim against the engrained belief in the guarantee of identity.

1 Jacques-Alain Miller quoted in Catherine Liu's online description of the event, "My Lacan is Burning: Revisiting 'Television'" (2004), organized by *Slought Foundation*, http://slought.org/content/11175/.

2 The interview was recorded and edited in October and November 1973 and later broadcast in March 1974. The book *Télévision* by Jacques Lacan was first published in French by Éditions du Seuil (Paris) in February 1974.

3 *Thirteen Shooters* was made in response to an invitation by the Queens Museum of Art in New York to create a new work based on another in their collection. Robert Beck chose Andy Warhol's *13 Most Wanted Men* (1964).

4 Myspace was launched in August 2003; Facebook was launched in February 2004; and YouTube was created in February 2005.

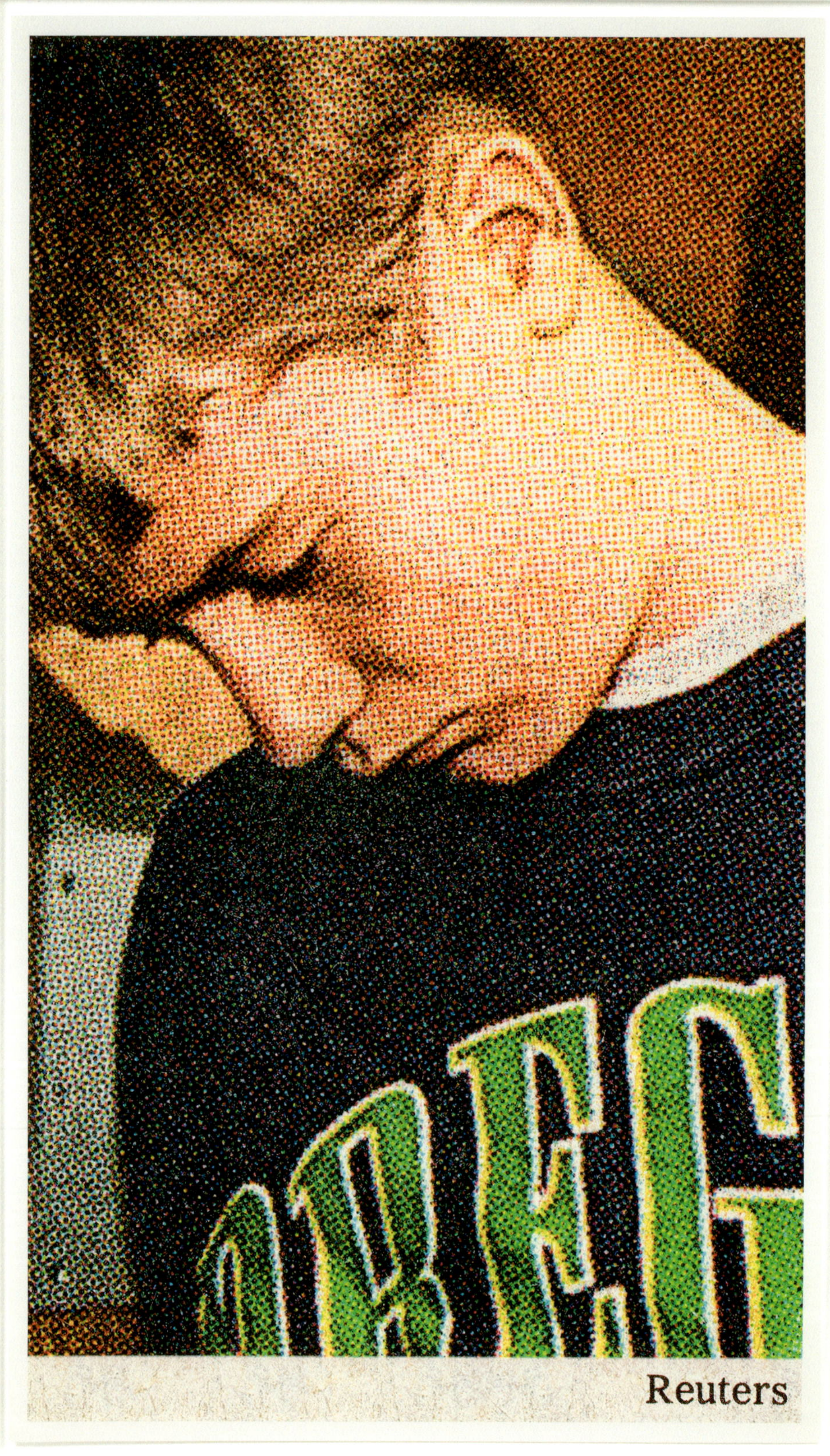
Reuters

« QUEL NOM VAIS-JE SIGNER? » : L'ART DE ROBERT BUCK

James Voorhies

Sur le trottoir près de l'entrée d'une galerie sur East Pender Street à Vancouver, en Colombie Britannique, les visiteurs de l'exposition d'œuvres de Robert Buck croisent un petit sanctuaire de fortune. Un ramassis éclectique d'animaux en peluche, de chandelles parfumées, de photos encadrées et de poèmes repose aux côtés d'œillets, de dahlias et de lis fraîchement coupés. Certaines fleurs ont été vaporisées de peinture fuchsia éclatant ou pourpre. D'autres sont en plastique. Des ballons en cellophane, un ange en plastique et un pot à fleurs en forme de biche s'intègre à cet ensemble disparate. Les démonstrations publiques de condoléances comme celle-ci s'improvisent en réaction à un décès prématuré, parfois sur le lieu même d'un accident de bicyclette ou de voiture. Ailleurs, ils représentent un deuil collectif à la suite d'une tragédie largement médiatisée, comme une tuerie dans une école élémentaire ou un cinéma de banlieue. Ce type d'autels commémoratifs était chose courante pendant les semaines qui ont suivi le massacre qui a coûté la vie à vingt jeunes écoliers et six adultes à l'école élémentaire Sandy Hook de Newtown, au Connecticut, en 2012. Le public des journaux télévisés et en ligne a pu voir en images l'éclosion de sanctuaires collectifs en réaction de sympathie partout dans le monde. Ces images illustraient des reportages qui tentaient de transmettre, voire d'humaniser, les événements. Même s'il porte à s'arrêter et à réfléchir, ce petit sanctuaire occupant le devant de cette galerie à Vancouver n'est malheureusement rien d'exceptionnel, dans une culture de violence de plus en plus répandue.

En entrant à l'exposition de Robert Buck à la galerie Rennie Collection, les visiteurs sont accueillis par le son régulier mais distinctif de coups de feu. Leur provenance est incertaine, dissimulée quelque part à l'arrière de la galerie. Mais les sons ajoutent à un malaise déjà ressenti devant le sanctuaire à l'extérieur. L'oeuvre *Untitled (Daly Over/Under @ Close Range w/.12 "Punkin' Ball" Slug) (Entrance and Exit)* (1999) est accrochée à droite de l'entrée. Il s'agit d'un diptyque composé de deux cahiers à dessin à reliure spirale. Un trou réalisé par une grosse balle de fusil perce le centre de chaque surface. Il fait environ 2,5 cm de diamètre et un dégradé de noir et de gris entoure son centre foncé. Des marques délicatement bigarrées semblent avoir été tracées par hasard avec des spores de champignon ou du pollen de fleurs. Le coup de feu tiré du

24 verso du cahier est propulsé vers l'extérieur à la manière d'une fleur naissante. Ces marques sont le produit d'actes violents, mais la beauté des surfaces semble paradoxale.

Sur le mur opposé, *A Part from the Whole (Communion)* (2005) regroupe onze photos dans un grand cadre en composite, du type bon marché que l'on utilise pour regrouper des photos de bal des finissants, de mariage ou de pique-nique familial. Il s'agit de photos recadrées de la première communion d'un jeune garçon et d'une jeune fille catholiques, notamment des gros plans de mains en prière ou tenant un recueil de chants. Des références au père et à la mère sont présentes dans quelques images. Dans une photo, l'ombre du père se projette sur le corps du garçon, laissant sa marque au moment précis de la prise de la photo. Dans une autre, la main du père entoure l'épaule du garçon et dans une autre encore, la mère tient des lunettes de soleil dans ses mains. Ce paysage visuel sous-jacent émerge des grandes images qui représentent des événements de l'enfance (que nous ne connaissons pas) dans des carrés, des rectangles et dans un unique cadre circulaire contenant la photo des mains du garçon en prière. Cette ouverture circulaire rappelle le *tondo* classique, tableau de forme ronde de la Renaissance, traditionnellement réservé aux portraits religieux représentant la mère et l'enfant. Alors que ces rituels symboliques de purification sont illustrés dans *Communion*, les gestes physiques de nettoyage sont gravés dans la surface d'*Untitled (Clean)* (2004), que l'on aperçoit tout près. Cette cloison de salle de toilettes en acier brillant, vissée directement sur le mur, interpelle les visiteurs à l'entrée de l'exposition. Sortie de sa fonction originale de séparation des toilettes publiques et d'orientation du comportement social, elle renvoie aux visiteurs leurs reflets fugitifs et flous, fondus parmi les diverses égratignures et taches de couleur.

Tandis que les coups de feu continuent de résonner dans la galerie, les visiteurs sont attirés vers l'intérieur. Ils peuvent ainsi voir le dessin grandeur nature *Two-Pin Toggle ("The Modern Man's Guide to Life" by Denise Boyles, Alan Rose, Alan Wellikoff)* (2001) à l'extrémité du corridor. Se servant du fusain sur une grande feuille de papier, l'artiste reproduit une illustration tirée du livre *The Modern Man's Guide to Life* (1987) qui explique aux lecteurs (vraisemblablement de jeunes adolescents) comment devenir un homme. Ce dessin est une version agrandie d'une illustration montrant la façon d'attraper de petits animaux. Le collet à bascule est une technique de piégeage consistant à enrouler deux petits morceaux de bois biseautés avec une corde et à les enfoncer dans le sol afin de fabriquer un collet. *Two-Pin Toggle* montre combien la masculinité est inscrite profondément très tôt dans la vie des jeunes garçons par le truchement d'un discours imprégné d'images et de langage.

En s'éloignant du dessin, les visiteurs découvrent l'installation vidéo *Untitled (Dec. 29, 1993)* (1999) dans un coin sombre derrière la cage d'escalier. C'est de cet endroit que proviennent les sons de coups de feu. Ils émanent de cette installation audiovisuelle anthropomorphique devant laquelle se tiennent les visiteurs, regardant directement l'écran noir et blanc dont émergent des cercles blancs concentriques rythmés qui rappellent la constriction et la dilatation d'une pupille ou d'un sphincter. Portant une date, le 29 décembre 1993, la vidéo résulte du travail d'une lentille automatique qui se recalibre constamment, à la recherche de son sujet, lequel demeure à jamais éphémère, car le capuchon demeure sur la lentille. Les spectateurs attendent impatiemment de voir une image représentative afin de combler leur dépendance désespérée à l'image pour comprendre toute chose. Or, les spectateurs doivent se contenter de cercles concentriques et hypnotiques d'énergie libidinale tandis qu'ils écoutent, très attentivement, les voix étouffées de deux hommes, entremêlées de grondements sourds causés par le vent soufflant dans le microphone. On peut entendre la voix impatiente d'un père montrant à son fils comment tirer au fusil, tandis que le fils lui explique comment utiliser un appareil-photo. Leurs brefs échanges portent sur la façon de tenir un fusil, de déterminer s'il est verrouillé et si l'appareil-photo est en marche ou non. Leurs paroles sont entrecoupées d'un silence inconfortable interrompu par ce son présent depuis le début de l'exposition : un coup de feu – plus fort et plus intense cette fois-ci.

I. [*Je dis toujours la vérité*]

Ces œuvres ont été conçues et réalisées par Robert Beck avant qu'il ne change son nom, en 2008, de Beck à Buck. Son geste défie toute catégorisation et va à l'encontre des mécanismes habituels d'identification d'un artiste par un style particulier, un médium et même un nom. Ses sculptures, dessins, peintures, textes, vidéos, installations et expositions s'approprient des formes familières – comme un sanctuaire de fortune et une illustration tirée d'un manuel d'instructions. L'artiste puise dans les croyances associées à ces formes afin de décourager les attentes qu'elles suscitent. Par exemple, les sanctuaires commémoratifs spontanés sont associés à l'évidence qu'une personne est décédée. Et, de ce fait, une personne a été touchée suffisamment pour souligner cet événement, puis d'autres aussi ont été touchés pour acheter, fabriquer ou déposer un objet en souvenir de cette personne. L'idée d'un sanctuaire improvisé sur le trottoir repose en partie sur la supposition que tout ceci est vrai. Le sanctuaire *The Shrine (from e to u)* (2000/2012), que les visiteurs croisent avant d'entrer dans la galerie, en donne toutes les apparences. Il invite au même comportement que tout autre sanctuaire improvisé : être perçu comme une réponse à un événement tragique.

26   Toutefois, dès que les gens se rendent compte que le sanctuaire ne commémore pas un événement réel, comme la tragédie de Sandy Hook, cette forme exprime alors une demi-vérité sur l'idée que l'on s'en fait. L'appropriation éclipse les hypothèses ancrées dans ces formes familières, et comme œuvres d'art, ces dernières deviennent des véhicules pouvant révéler en premier lieu les répercussions politiques et sociales globales liées à leur existence.

Toutefois, l'aspect politique dans l'art de Robert Buck n'est pas une critique évidente du contrôle des armes à feu, par exemple. L'art de Buck ne cherche pas à porter des jugements précis dans ces conditions. Nous n'apprenons pas sa position sur les armes à feu et, en fait, nous devons nous questionner à savoir s'il est important de connaître ce point de vue pour réagir à l'oeuvre. En recadrant et en remettant en contexte l'aspect familier, Buck porte l'aspect politique de son art à émerger sous des formes reposant sur l'expérience de la réalité vécue par les visiteurs et sur leur compréhension des phénomènes, et il le juxtapose dans une topologie qui trace un processus d'interprétation physique et mental de l'exposition en la parcourant et en l'examinant, même si cela mène sur le trottoir à l'extérieur de la galerie. Buck organise l'exposition comme une topologie dans le but de rassembler les demi-vérités inhérentes que les œuvres individuelles révèlent. *The Shrine* n'a pas plus de portée politique qu'un autre sanctuaire de fortune, à moins qu'il ne soit intégré dans le monde de l'art et interprété en relation avec d'autres œuvres d'une exposition, comme la vidéo *Dec. 29, 1993*, la photographie *Communion* et le dessin *Two-Pin Toggle*. Lorsque ces œuvres sont abordées en relation les unes avec les autres, elles se lisent comme un texte où chaque signifiant-objet d'art devient l'élément d'une phrase explorant l'effet de balayage que les institutions sociales, comme la famille, la race, la sexualité, la religion, les médias, l'éducation et la langue, ont sur la politique et la culture – notre mode de vie actuel. Ce mariage de la familiarité et de la confusion s'appuie sur cet aspect unique d'une politique d'esthétique en modifiant l'apparence des choses et en repositionnant nos perspectives. Et c'est là que se trouve l'aspect critique. C'est-à-dire ce qui a le potentiel de changer les perceptions et de générer une nouvelle compréhension du monde. Ainsi, à la sortie de la galerie, les visiteurs ont une tout autre interprétation de *The Shrine*.

Je dis toujours la vérité : pas toute,
parce que toute la dire, on n'y arrive pas. La dire toute,
c'est impossible, matériellement : les mots y manquent. C'est même par
cet impossible que la vérité tient au réel.

Ces paroles sont celles du psychanalyste français Jacques Lacan lors d'une entrevue télévisée. En janvier 1973, le jeune universitaire et futur psychanalyste, Jacques-Alain Miller, a demandé à Lacan de se prêter à l'entrevue parce qu'il « voulait que Lacan, juste une fois, parle à l'homme ordinaire[1] ». Diffusée initialement sous le titre « Psychanalyse » sur un réseau d'État français, l'émission en deux parties a été publiée simultanément dans un livre intitulé *Télévision*, qui est le cadre directeur du présent texte sur l'art de Robert Buck[2]. Le livre *Télévision* est divisé en sept sections et, comme l'émission télévisée, regorge de réponses ludiques, de commentaires énigmatiques, de réflexions sérieuses et de déclarations incongrues de Lacan, qui illustrent la « comédie », selon ses mots, consistant à résumer la psychanalyse. En effet, sa présence surprenante, curieuse et teintée de satire à l'écran révèle une conscience de la tâche impossible, voire même ridicule, de parler en général de la pratique de la psychanalyse au grand public. Toutefois, tout au long de l'entrevue, il fait exactement ce qu'on lui demande : il joue le rôle du psychanalyste.

La théorie psychanalytique de Jacques Lacan reprend les concepts freudiens. Mais contrairement à Freud, pour Lacan la conscience n'a rien à voir avec la psychanalyse. Au début de sa carrière, Lacan considérait la psychanalyse comme un moyen pour lire, constater et accepter l'inconscient, tel qu'il est. L'axiome fondamental de Lacan est que l'inconscient est structuré comme un langage. Or, cela peut sembler paradoxal : le langage est aussi ce qui permet à une lecture de l'inconscient et donc à un discours psychanalytique de vraiment exister. Par conséquent, même si l'inconscient ne peut jamais être totalement élucidé ou résolu, il peut être approché par le truchement de ses traces — les lapsus, plaisanteries, actes manqués, rêves. Les occurrences de l'inconscient qui émergent dans la réalité sont des demi-vérités ayant la structure de la fiction qui prennent une forme et une signification par le truchement d'un dialogue entre un analyste et un sujet. Cet échange est fondé sur un langage qui se manifeste par la libre association et dans le discours de l'être parlant. Par conséquent, l'analyse est une réflexion critique du discours, ou des liens sociaux, dans lequel le sujet humain n'a pas d'autre choix que de parler, comme l'exprime les traces de l'inconscient, qui encode et traite chaque moment jour après jour. La prestation télévisée de Lacan nous promettait une position sur la psychanalyse, mais elle a plutôt contribué au bris de cette promesse, car elle a été en réalité un constat d'échec. Et cet échec traduisait l'impossibilité logique de communiquer une explication de l'inconscient et de définir la psychanalyse adéquatement.

Car il n'y a pas de différence entre la télévision et le
public devant lequel je parle depuis longtemps,
ce qu'on appelle mon séminaire. Un regard dans les deux
cas : à qui je ne m'adresse dans aucun,
mais au nom de quoi je parle.

À l'exposition des œuvres de Buck, les visiteurs empruntent un escalier pour atteindre une salle au premier étage. Ils entrent alors dans un espace immense doté de murs de 11,8 m de hauteur où la série photographique *Thirteen Shooters* (2001) s'étend du plancher au plafond[3]. La vaste salle d'une superficie de 17,8 m par 9 m combinée aux plafonds imposants revêt les allures d'une cathédrale, accentuées par l'arrière-plan absidal composé des photos de jeunes garçons. Les treize impressions en format affiche des portraits individuels d'adolescents utilisent des images photographiques et un texte appropriés d'autres sources. Notre attention est attirée immédiatement vers l'intérieur et le haut, vers cet autel-sanctuaire dont la disposition banale suggère des images tombant du ciel ou défilant sur l'écran d'un ordinateur. Les portraits imposent – en fait, exigent – une force visuelle extraordinaire sur l'expérience de l'espace tout entier. Les photos sont composées de points Ben-Day et de couleurs, et sont tirées de divers journaux; certaines sont des photos plus officielles d'album de finissants ou des photos personnelles prises à des événements sportifs ou des réunions de famille. D'autres proviennent vraiment des médias, qu'elles aient été prises durant les audiences ou à la sortie du tribunal. Beck ajoute une légende à chaque image, mais elle ne révèle pas les noms et prénoms des garçons. Ils sont plutôt remplacés par les noms des médias ou des photographes : Reuters, Corbis Sygma, Associated Press, Elaine Thomas – AP et San Diego Union-Tribune. En face, au centre et confrontant le regard du visiteur, on trouve un diptyque des photos d'Eric Harris et Dylan Klebold; ce sont les mêmes photos qui ont fait le tour du monde sur les écrans de télévision à la fin des années 1990, après la tragédie de Columbine, et qui sont aujourd'hui archivées en permanence dans Wikipédia. Dans cette installation, ces portraits agissent comme des forces centrifuges vers lesquelles gravitent les autres photos des jeunes tueurs.

Même si chaque photographie de *Thirteen Shooters* présente un garçon différent, la diversité et la portée des types de portraits illustrent l'identité singulière du tueur adolescent tristement célèbre interprétée par les médias. Autrement dit, quelques heures seulement après un massacre, des photos du tueur dans une garderie, une école primaire, à un match de soccer ou un bal des finissants sont invariablement destinées au grand public. Les jours suivants, s'ajoutent d'autres photos de l'interpellation et de la condamnation. Les médias modèlent et formulent une identité composite d'un tueur en diffusant ces types d'image avec rapidité et précision.

Alors que Beck tait les noms des garçons photographiés dans *Thirteen Shooters*, la sculpture *Artwork by Kip Kinkel for His Parents Bill and Faith* (2004), dans la même salle, affiche les noms véritables, l'artiste voulant explorer les effets combinés de la famille et des médias sur la création d'une identité. En Oregon en 1998, dans une fusillade meurtrière, Kip Kinkel tue sa mère, son père et deux camarades de l'école secondaire. *Artwork* combine les formes courantes du paillasson et du tapis de bain, chacun étant moulé et présenté comme une pierre tombale. Ces sculptures sont faites de silicone blanche. Sept trous de balle moulés dans un matériau cireux de remplissage des plaies des corps embaumés afin d'être exposés sont répartis sur les deux surfaces. Le nombre de trous correspond aux balles tirées par Kinkel sur ses parents : six sur sa mère et une sur son père.

Non loin, le texte et l'image s'entrecroisent aussi dans une série de dessins « diagnostiques » exécutés par Beck. Les dessins s'inspirent de divers tests de personnalité publiés, dont le test *House-Tree-Person* (HTP), élaboré par le psychologue John N. Buck dans les années 1960. Les sujets sont invités à dessiner les objets mentionnés précédemment dans le test puis à répondre à une liste exhaustive de questions portant sur leurs dessins. L'évaluation qualitative du patient est fondée sur une interprétation subjective de leurs réponses et des images. Ces œuvres de Beck combinent des dessins réels de patients et des commentaires de leurs analystes, tous reproduits de la main de l'artiste. Beck utilise de la poudre pour empreintes digitales latentes, dont se sert la police sur les scènes de crime, afin de remplir les différentes sections en arrière-plan et de laisser des traces de doigts.

La salle contient également la sculpture *01/25/04 – Shots No. 12, 13, 14 (Daly Over/Under at Close Range with .12 Gauge "Punkin' Ball" Slug)* (2004). Elle est composée de trois seaux de 25 gallons en plastique, débordant de produit de remplissage des plaies de couleur chair. De la même façon que dans le tableau *Entrance and Exit,* Beck a tiré à bout portant un coup de feu dans chaque seau, cette fois-ci profondément dans la substance semblable à de la graisse, laissant un trou béant dans le matériau passant par-dessus le rebord circulaire. La substance même qui est employée pour réparer les plaies adopte ici une qualité corporelle, perforée mais en fait irréparable. À l'opposé de *Thirteen Shooters* on peut voir *'ccused of K (The New York Times, Nov 30, 2002)* (2003), une reproduction de 2,6 m par 2,1 m d'un jeune adolescent au regard taquin et aux magnifiques cheveux bouclés, qui fixe tristement le visiteur. L'image est tirée d'un article de journal portant sur les deux frères King – Alex et Derek – qui ont été accusés et condamnés en 2001 du meurtre de leur père qui dormait dans un fauteuil La-z-boy. Beck a méticuleusement reproduit à la main une section de l'article. Ces œuvres traitent d'une culture d'adulation qui ne se limite pas qu'aux vedettes de cinéma, aux idoles d'adolescents et aux icônes du sport, et où les leçons de masculinité explorées dans *Two-Pin Toggle* et *Dec. 29, 1993* tournent mal.

Le langage structure notre réalité. Pour Lacan, l'inconscient est une chose précise parce qu'il se manifeste dans les éventualités que nous impose le langage. Par le discours et à cause du discours, nous ne pouvons réaliser totalement notre désir et il en reste toujours quelque chose dans l'inconscient. Cette immersion dans le langage est à la fois un facteur permissif et prohibitif dans nos négociations entre la vie quotidienne et l'inconscient, car le langage ne peut jamais transmettre complètement ce que nous voulons qu'il dise et fasse. Dans la prise en considération de la fonction du langage, la théorie de l'ordre symbolique avancée par Lacan est souvent appelée le « Nom du père ». Selon cette théorie, qui reformule la vision freudienne du complexe d'Oedipe, la loi sociétale est déterminée – littéralement et métaphoriquement – par le nom du père. Notre nom vient de cette loi paternelle, qui est le fondement même de notre apprentissage à nommer et à comprendre le monde. C'est la première expérience que nous avons du langage, et cette rencontre initiale est déterminée par les circonstances familiales, le désir envers la mère et le « non » du père. Pour Lacan, c'est par la fonction paternelle du langage que le comportement social est ordonné. Toutefois, il a par la suite repensé la loi paternelle en la nommant « Noms du père » au pluriel afin de refléter sa fonction unique pour chacun d'entre nous. Changer son nom peut entraîner la création de nouveaux liens au-delà de ceux qui régissent les forces familiales. Les nouvelles constellations reconfigurent l'existence du sujet dans le langage, ouvrant de nouvelles possibilités d'annuler ses effets contraignants, reconstitués par le geste symbolique du changement de nom. Comme invention, ce geste est une récupération et une réorientation du désir.

III. [*Être un saint*]

Dans la salle adjacente à celle où se trouve *Thirteen Shooters*, l'ordre familial est un thème prédominant. On peut voir, installée au centre de cet espace, la sculpture *Wall Ceiling ("Bless This House…")* (2004). L'œuvre consiste en une section transversale provenant d'un ensemble architectural plus vaste. Un mur isolé, inversé, tient à la verticale et le plafond forme un angle droit avec le mur, le tout semblant avoir été extrait avec la plus grande précision. La qualité modeste, voire bon marché, du mur et du plafond renvoie aux innombrables salles de jeux des banlieues populaires américaines. La remise en contexte par Beck de cette architecture commune est une contestation ludique des valeurs associées à l'identité familiale américaine et de la stabilité matérielle et symbolique qui y est associée. Un poème dans un cadre est accroché à l'envers au mur : « Bless this house/Oh Lord we pray/Make it safe/By night and day. » (Bénis cette demeure/Seigneur nous te prions/Protège-la/Jour et nuit.)

Cinq photographies granuleuses grand format sont installées sur le pourtour de cette salle et rayonnent avec une intensité bienveillante autour de *Wall Ceiling* et des visiteurs. Ces épreuves à la gélatine argentique noir et blanc sont intitulées *Screen Memory* (2004) et comportent un sous-titre entre parenthèses, soit *Father's Room*, *Mother's Room*, *Brother's Room*, *Sister's Room* et *Family Room*. Le titre de la série fait référence à la théorie des souvenirs d'enfance avancée par Freud, selon laquelle des détails apparemment insignifiants servent de substituts ou d'écrans à des expériences et des événements plus significatifs de l'enfance. Chaque photographie présente des réflexions superposées de différents lieux domestiques qui se transforment en portraits substituts des membres d'une famille. *Mother's Room*, par exemple, présente l'image iconique de JésusChrist regardant pieusement vers le bas; des rideaux sombres sont partiellement ouverts et se reflètent dans le verre de la reproduction bon marché. *Father's Room* présente la photo de deux oies prenant leur envol, tandis que des volets à travers lesquels le soleil de l'après-midi filtre dans une pièce poussiéreuse apparaissent dans son reflet. Bien que *Mother's Room* soit accroché très près de *Father's Room*, les tableaux sont installés sur des murs distincts. *Brother's Room* présente un aigle et le drapeau américain; dans *Sister's Room*, c'est l'image d'une licorne qui domine. La pièce pour l'artiste, toutefois, est manifestement absente.

J'interpole ici une remarque. Je ne fonde pas
cette idée de discours sur l'ex-sistence de
l'inconscient. C'est l'inconscient que
j'en situe, – de n'exister qu'à un discours.

IV. [*Ces gestes vagues dont de mon discours on se garantit.*]

L'œuvre *dust (Community Times, June 20, 1965)* (1998/2006) de Beck occupe un étroit corridor de 17,8 m de long par 1,4 m de large qui sépare deux salles. Dans cet environnement immersif

32   et restreint, un mur de 13 m est peint du plancher jusqu'au plafond avec de la peinture ardoise afin de créer une surface de tableau noir. On peut y voir, écrits à la main sur tout le mur, des textes – articles, publicités, nécrologie et petites annonces – tirés d'un numéro du *Community Times*, qui était l'hebdomadaire de la ville natale de l'artiste, daté du 20 juin 1965. La plupart des mots sont effacés, créant un filtre diffus à travers lequel le visiteur promène son regard sur la surface, tout en se déplaçant dans l'espace afin de saisir le sens des textes partiellement effacés. La charge symbolique et réelle lancée par Beck contre notre façon de savoir et d'exister dans le monde s'inspire des expériences avec l'éducation et les médias tout en les rassemblant. À cette convergence de la salle de classe et du journal, une petite photo Polaroid encadrée est ajoutée sur le mur. La photo évoque la mort au sens littéral dans l'image d'une pierre tombale d'enfant, qui attire les visiteurs dans ce corridor où la religion, l'éducation, les souvenirs et les médias s'entrechoquent dans un moment unique d'immersion.

dust est à la fois la construction et la dégradation du langage; un geste physique contre les filtres d'interprétation et de modification qui orientent et définissent notre compréhension du monde, de l'adolescence à la vie adulte. Ainsi, nous sommes devant ce mur de langage imposant où le texte partiellement effacé reflète une vérité comprise par le truchement de ce qui est présent autant qu'absent dans les modes superposés du souvenir et de l'oubli.

Ainsi l'affect vient-il à un corps dont le propre serait
d'habiter le langage – je me geaite ici de plumes
qui se vendent mieux que les miennes –, l'affect, dis-je,
de ne pas trouver de
logement, pas de son goût tout au moins.

V. [*Ce savoir en tant qu'il ne pense.*]

La preuve de l'effacement est à jamais marquée sur la surface de *Wall Hung Urinal Screen ("Big Red")* (2003) : une cloison de cabine de toilettes qui, tout comme *Untitled (Clean)*, est retirée d'un lieu qui contient des divisions séparant des corps masculins dans des toilettes publiques. Ici, dans la galerie, cette cloison devient une peinture-sculpture abstraite accrochée perpendiculairement au mur que les visiteurs doivent aborder d'une manière différente. La précision avec laquelle l'artiste a reproduit la forme jette un certain doute quant à sa place comme œuvre d'art ou artéfact. Sur la peinture-émail blanc cassé on peut lire des phases comme

« Jerk Off », « MOTHERFUCKINGMINT », « SEX ME MOMMY » et « BIG RED ». Cette
dernière expression est gravée à côté du dessin d'un énorme pénis. Ces mots sont visibles dans le
contexte de *Mother's Room* et *Father's Room* situés dans la salle adjacente et dans des perspectives
opposées. Ces actes transgressifs sont chose commune dans les toilettes des écoles secondaires où
les garçons affrontent continuellement la direction de l'école quant à l'utilisation des murs pour
diffuser un discours non censuré. De source anonyme, les textes et les images dans les toilettes
publiques – même si elles sont temporaires – symbolisent l'assouvissement d'un désir latent sans
le fardeau habituel de la censure sociétale.

*C'est là notre chance que nous en touchions le réel pur et simple, – comme
ce qui empêche d'en dire toute la vérité.*

Hidden Pictures (At Rest) (2004) est installé dans la même salle. Il s'agit d'un dessin à la mine de
plomb sur papier de 1,2 m par 2,8 m, inspiré de la page *Hidden Pictures* du magazine américain
pour enfants *Highlights*. Fonctionnant à un niveau diagnostique moins formel que les tests de
personnalité *House-Tree-Person*, le journal mensuel lancé dans les années 1940 contenait des pages
de bricolage, des plaisanteries, des casse-tête et des jeux éducatifs pour les enfants, qui devaient
chercher entre les traits d'un dessin des objets au hasard, comme un stylo à bille ou un poisson,
définis par les contours de scènes plus vastes comme une ferme ou un marché aux légumes.
Hidden Pictures (At Rest) est créé à partir d'une page intitulée *Corn City*, ou Cité du maïs, ville
imaginaire construite entièrement en épis de maïs. Dans le texte explicatif, on demande aux
enfants de chercher, entre autres, un bonhomme de neige, un palmier, une chandelle, un foulard,
un feu de camp et un garçon. Beck a tout effacé sauf une image dans la grande illustration. C'est
le corps d'un enfant couché dans l'ornière d'un chemin, comme s'il avait été exhumé. On peut
difficilement s'attendre à trouver ce « garçon » dans un jeu pour enfants. À droite de la scène
s'étend plus d'un mètre de papier vierge, un espace vide invitant à voir en vain quelque indice
contribuant à clarifier ce scénario énigmatique. Alors que les dessins diagnostiques cherchaient un
sens dans les textes et les images, rien ici ne permet d'expliquer cette scène déstabilisante, qui est
extraite – ou mise en relief – à partir du tableau général.

*Qui ne sait que c'est du discours analytique
que j'ai fait fortune? En quoi je suis un
self-made man.*

En 1974, Lacan a exécuté un refus d'identité à la télévision. Sa présence à l'écran promettait d'offrir une définition de la psychanalyse. Or, il s'est abstenu essentiellement d'offrir une explication simple et rapide au grand public, car il refusait de réduire un ensemble complexe d'idées et de connaissances à une seule explication. En 2008, l'artiste Robert Beck a changé son nom pour Robert Buck. Les artistes aussi exécutent différentes fonctions attendues afin de satisfaire divers citoyens, notamment les marchands d'art, les collectionneurs, les musées, les salons d'art, les universitaires et les critiques. Ces citoyens forment l'« institution de l'art » qui formule des demandes à l'artiste. L'artiste représente un capital humain. Et ce capital humain est constitué et maintenu par le truchement d'une prestation publique continue de l'identité, c'est-à-dire les conférences, les expositions, l'écriture, les voyages, les relations sociales et l'enseignement. Ces prestations contribuent à la perception générale de l'artiste et l'aident à conserver une valeur économique et culturelle, à demeurer d'actualité et à se légitimer comme artiste.

Les artistes participent à la prestation de ce discours. Chez un artiste en milieu de carrière comme Beck, une infrastructure considérable était déjà construite autour de cette identité − la marque « Robert Beck » − et de cette prestation présumée. La transformation de l'artiste Robert Beck à l'artiste Robert Buck se voulait une contestation de ce discours, perturbant et décentralisant l'institution de l'art qui tente de contrecarrer ce genre de contestation en cherchant à perpétuer la singularité et la subjectivité, ancrées dans la croyance voulant qu'un nom soit une identité incarnée dans la signature d'un artiste.

L'attention extraordinaire portée à la création et au maintien de l'identité individuelle ne se limite pas qu'au monde de l'art. Du début jusqu'au milieu des années 2000, nous avons pu constater l'emphase sans précédent sur le marketing de l'identité individuelle et sur la personnalisation des avatars numériques. Les noms d'entreprises (sans compter les fonctions) comme Myspace, YouTube et Facebook indiquent que l'individu passe avant tout[4]. Actuellement, les courriels et les articles dans les réseaux sociaux sont recueillis puis analysés dans des algorithmes qui nous attribuent des choix de consommation que nous avons déjà mentionnés dans les informations que nous divulguons. La technologie façonne et affine constamment nos habitudes de consommation par le truchement des mots que nous écrivons dans Gmail, de nos achats sur Amazon, de nos visionnements sur Netflix et de la musique que nous écoutons sur iTunes. On doit aussi prendre en considération le nombre d'artistes dont le nom est suivi du suffixe « .com » dans les adresses de site Web et de courriel, et qui attribue en soi une valeur commerciale à l'identité de l'artiste. À une époque où l'identité fait l'objet d'une attention incessante, en particulier chez l'individu consommateur de tous les produits – éducation, mode, information, images et santé – nous devenons les proies des particularités qu'on nous attribue.

L'artiste s'épanouit dans ces circonstances historiques et commerciales complexes qui sont accentuées par l'institution de l'art. Le capital est un organisme inextricablement lié au désir humain. La société contemporaine est alimentée par des systèmes de production et de consommation où le capital exploite nos désirs afin de progresser, tout comme Freud a lancé l'hypothèse voulant que le principe de plaisir soit la pulsion libidinale sous-jacente de chacune de nos décisions et actions. L'artiste doit se présenter devant le public de diverses façons afin de communiquer avec le consommateur et de le toucher. Par les réalisations de l'effacement, de la modification et des demi-vérités, le changement de nom de Robert Buck défie les conditions liées à l'identité de l'artiste, jetant une ombre sur les structures gouvernant l'art et le langage qui définissent l'état d'artiste.

Faut-il que je revienne sur ce qu'il ne se situe véritablement
que d'un discours, soit ce dont l'artifice fait le concret?

VII. [*Ce qui s'énonce bien, l'on le conçoit clairement.*]

« Quel nom dois-je signer? » écrit James Joyce à sa bien-aimée Nora Barnacle à la fin d'une lettre datant de 1904. L'incertitude associée à cette question simple révèle une connaissance entendue des limites du langage et de son pouvoir sur la détermination de l'identité. Manifestement, la même question se pose tout au long de cette exposition de Robert Buck dans laquelle les œuvres rassemblées explorent différents processus d'identité, en commençant par les dessins diagnostiques, *Thirteen Shooters* et *dust* jusqu'à *Hidden Pictures*, aux photographies de *Screen Memory* et à la série lithographique *How Am I to Sign Myself* (2008), dont le titre est tiré de la question chimérique de Joyce. *How Am I to Sign Myself* de Robert Buck est une composition graphique en vingt-quatre parties qui contient les noms des visiteurs de l'exposition du même nom à la CRG Gallery de New York en 2007, soit sa dernière exposition à titre de Robert Beck. Utilisant la forme toute faite de la lettre à en-tête de son galeriste et l'immanquable livre de visiteurs, Buck s'approprie les noms des visiteurs, attirant l'attention sur la présentation périodique d'un ensemble d'œuvres au grand public. *How Am I to Sign Myself*, la première œuvre après le changement de nom de Beck

36   à Buck, révèle la liste des visiteurs de l'exposition identifiés par leurs signatures. Contrairement à l'absence notée dans les photographies de *Screen Memory*, ici l'artiste affirme sa présence avec la signature « R. Buck ». Tout comme la lettre de Joyce à sa bien-aimée se termine par la phrase « Je ne signerai rien du tout, parce que je ne sais pas quel nom signer », le simple changement de nom de Robert Buck « du e au u » (*from e to u*) vient ébranler la croyance enracinée dans la garantie d'identité.

1   Traduction de Jacques-Alain Miller cité dans la description en ligne par Catherine Liu de l'événement *My Lacan is Burning: Revisiting 'Television'* (2004), organisé par la *Slought Foundation*, http://slought.org content/11175/.

2   Cette entrevue a été enregistrée et montée en octobre et novembre 1973 puis diffusée en mars 1974. Le livre *Télévision* par Jacques Lacan a été publié pour la première fois en français aux Éditions du Seuil (Paris) en février 1974.

3   *Thirteen Shooters* a été réalisée en réponse à une invitation du Queens Museum of Art de New York à créer une œuvre à partir d'une autre œuvre de la collection. Robert Beck a choisi *13 Most Wanted Men* (1964) d'Andy Warhol.

4   Myspace a été lancé en août 2003; Facebook a été lancé en février 2004; et YouTube a été créé en février 2005.

 # AUTHOR'S BIOGRAPHY

JAMES VOORHIES is a curator, art historian and writer. He is John R. and Barbara Robinson Family Director of the Carpenter Center for the Visual Arts at Harvard University.

BIOGRAPHIE D'AUTEUR

JAMES VOORHIES est commissaire, historien de l'art et écrivain. Il est John R. and Barbara Robinson Family Directeur du Carpenter Center for the Visual Arts de Harvard University.

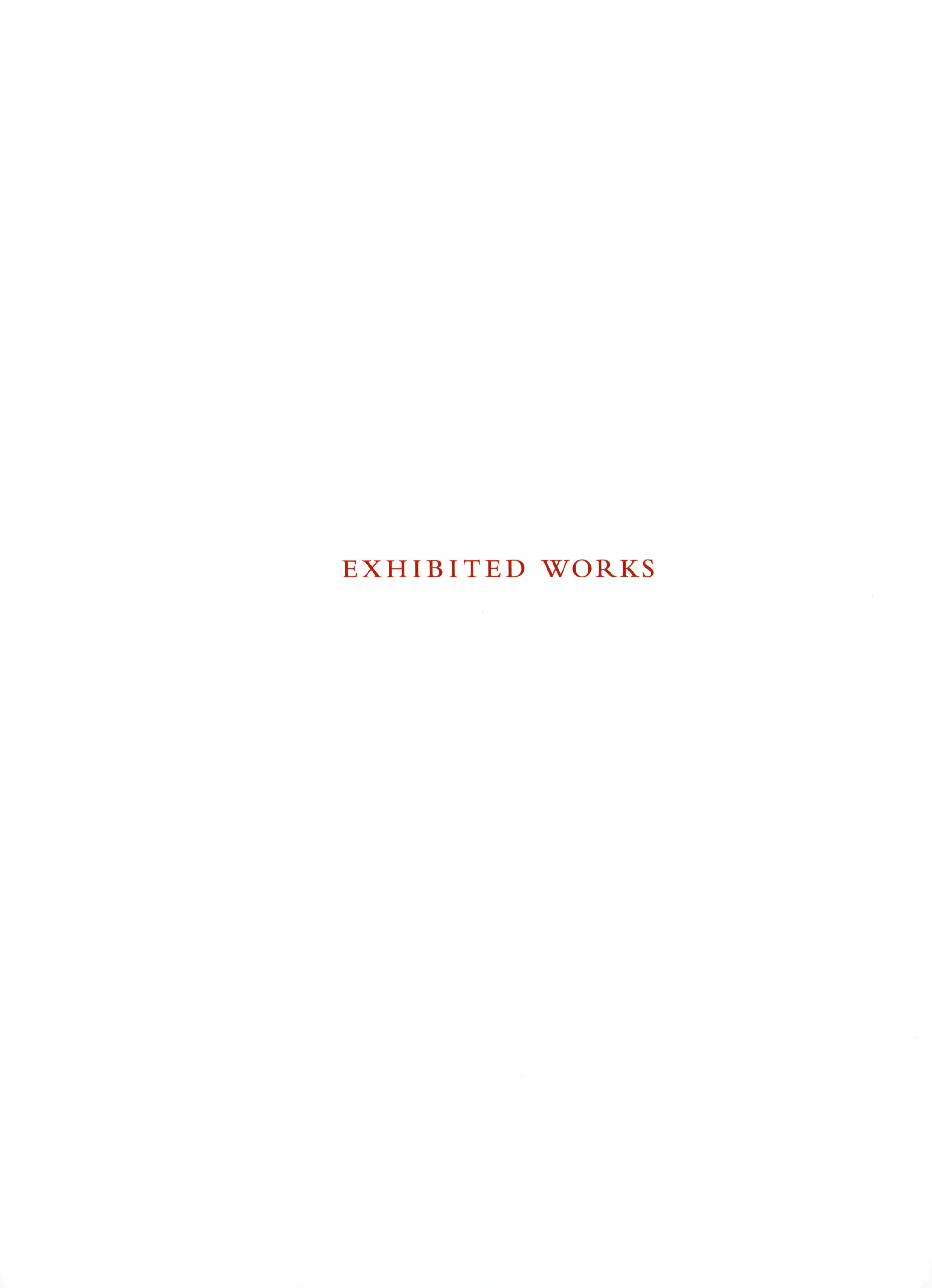

EXHIBITED WORKS

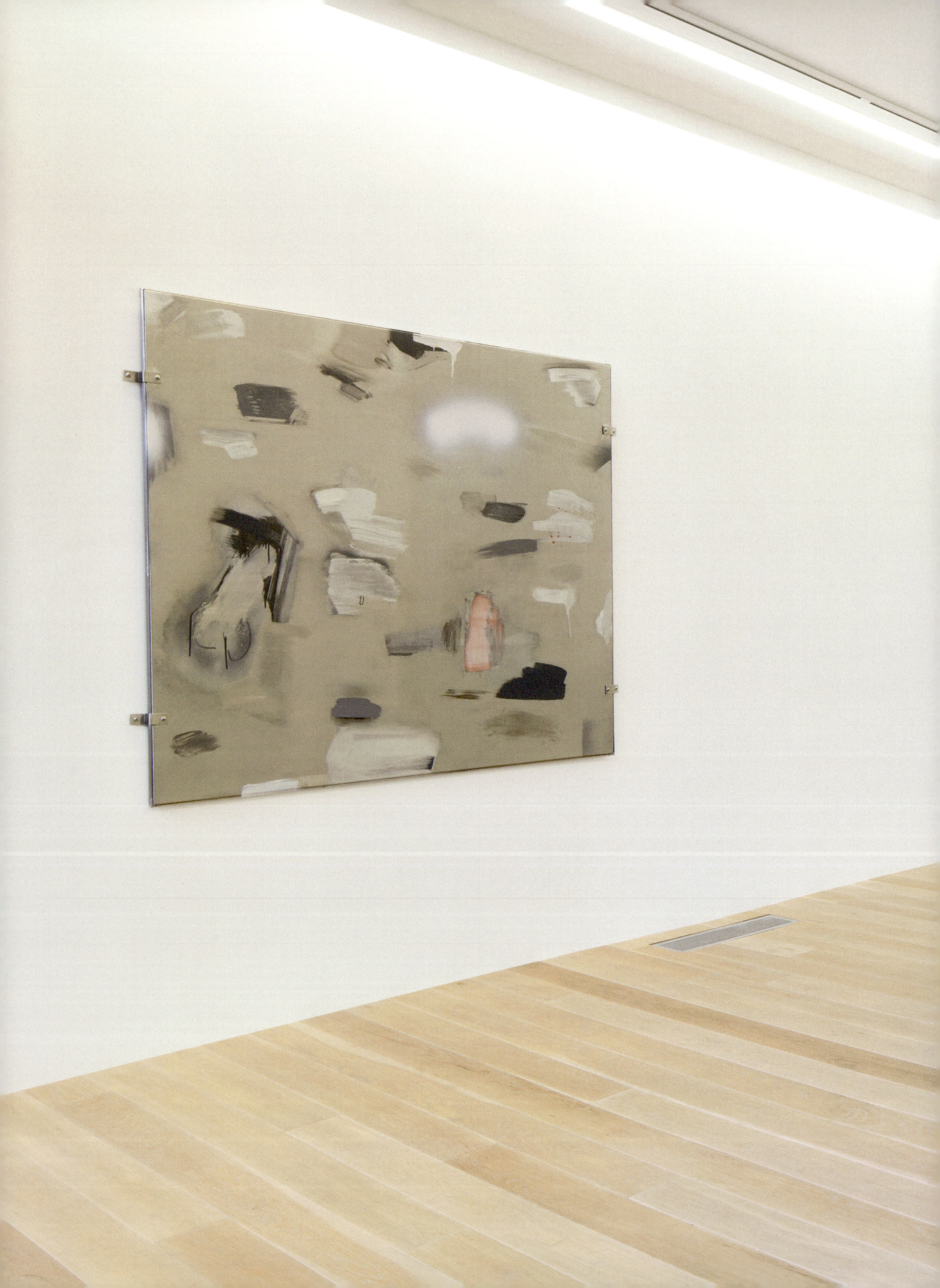

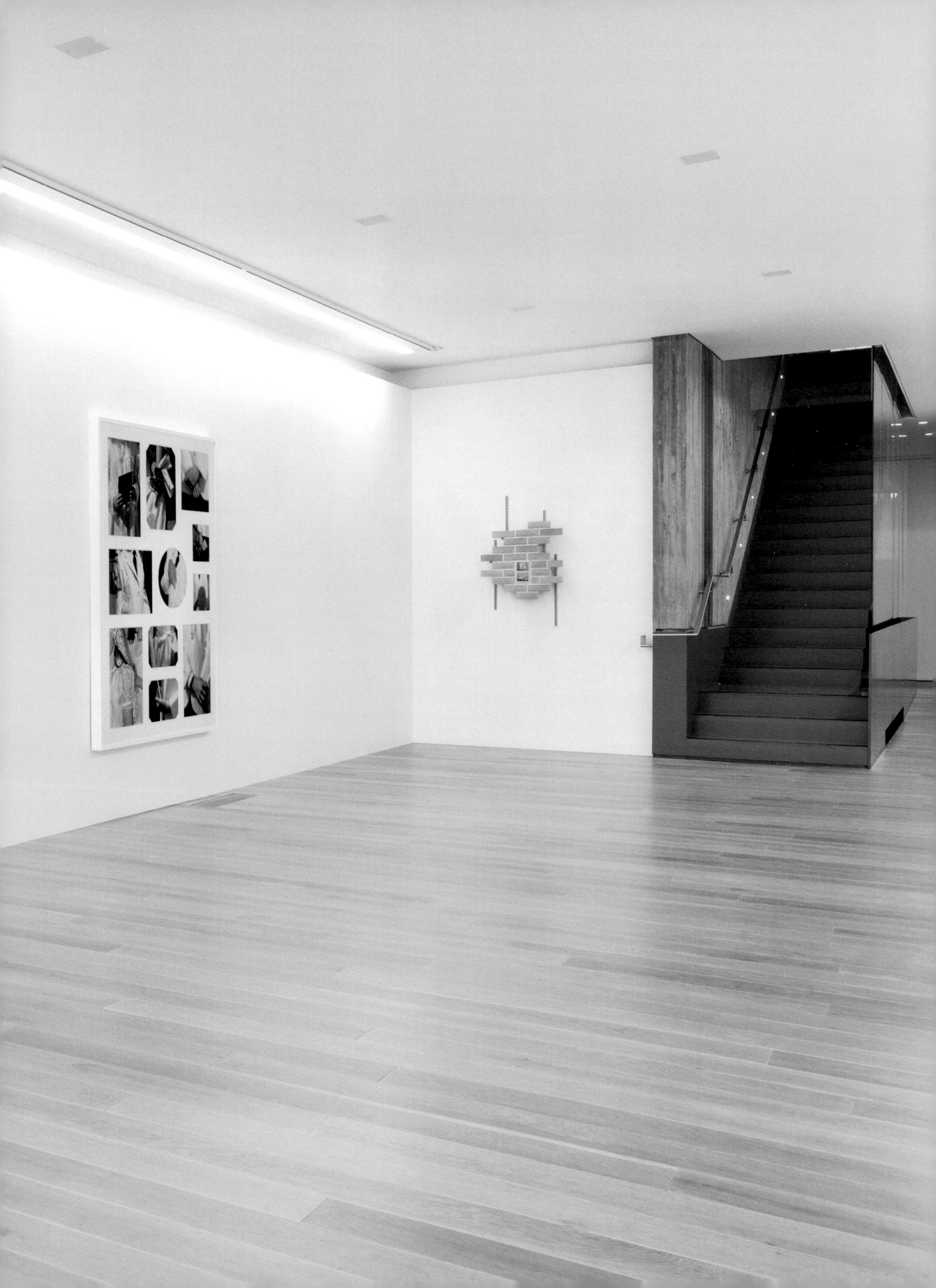

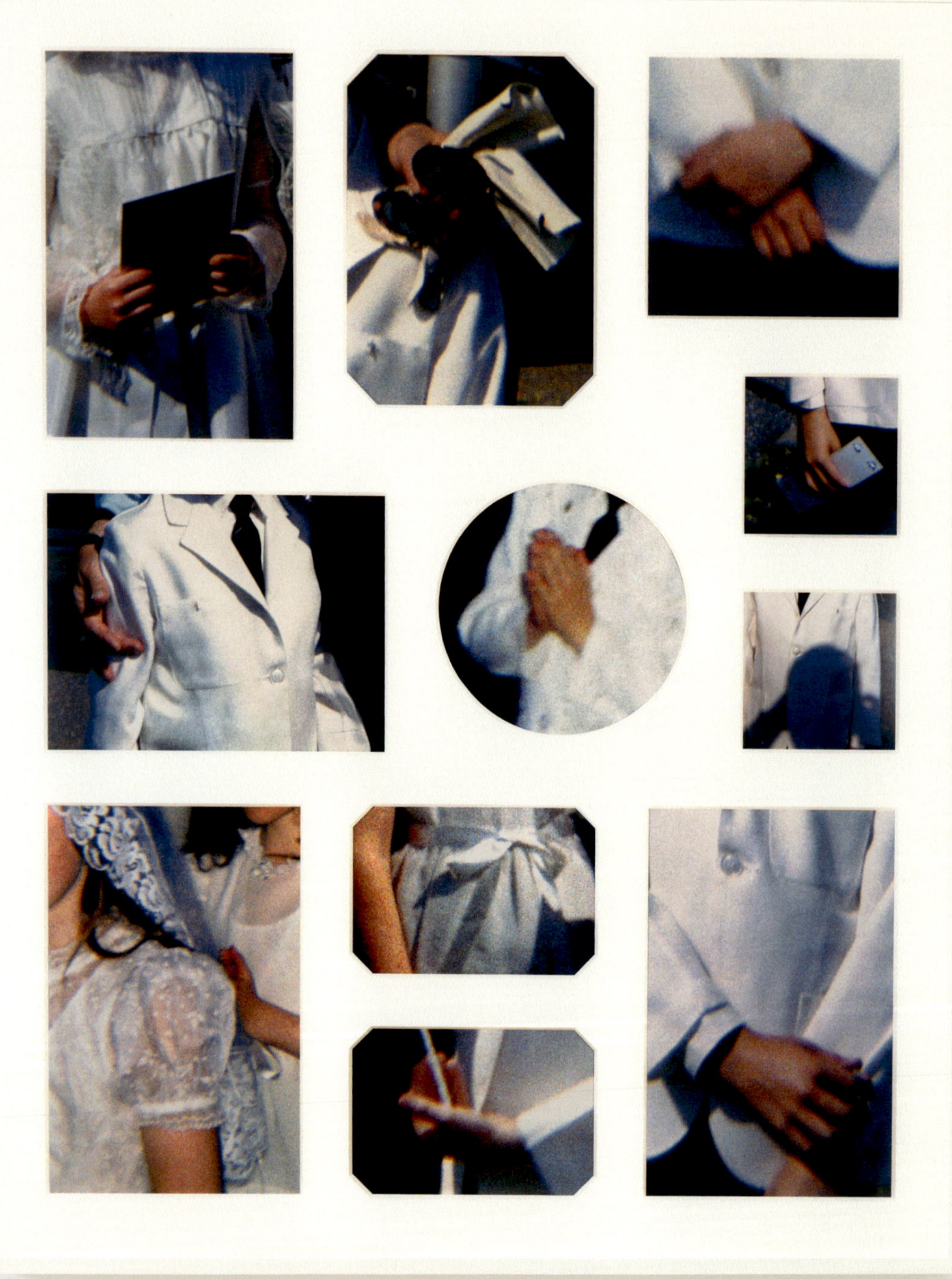

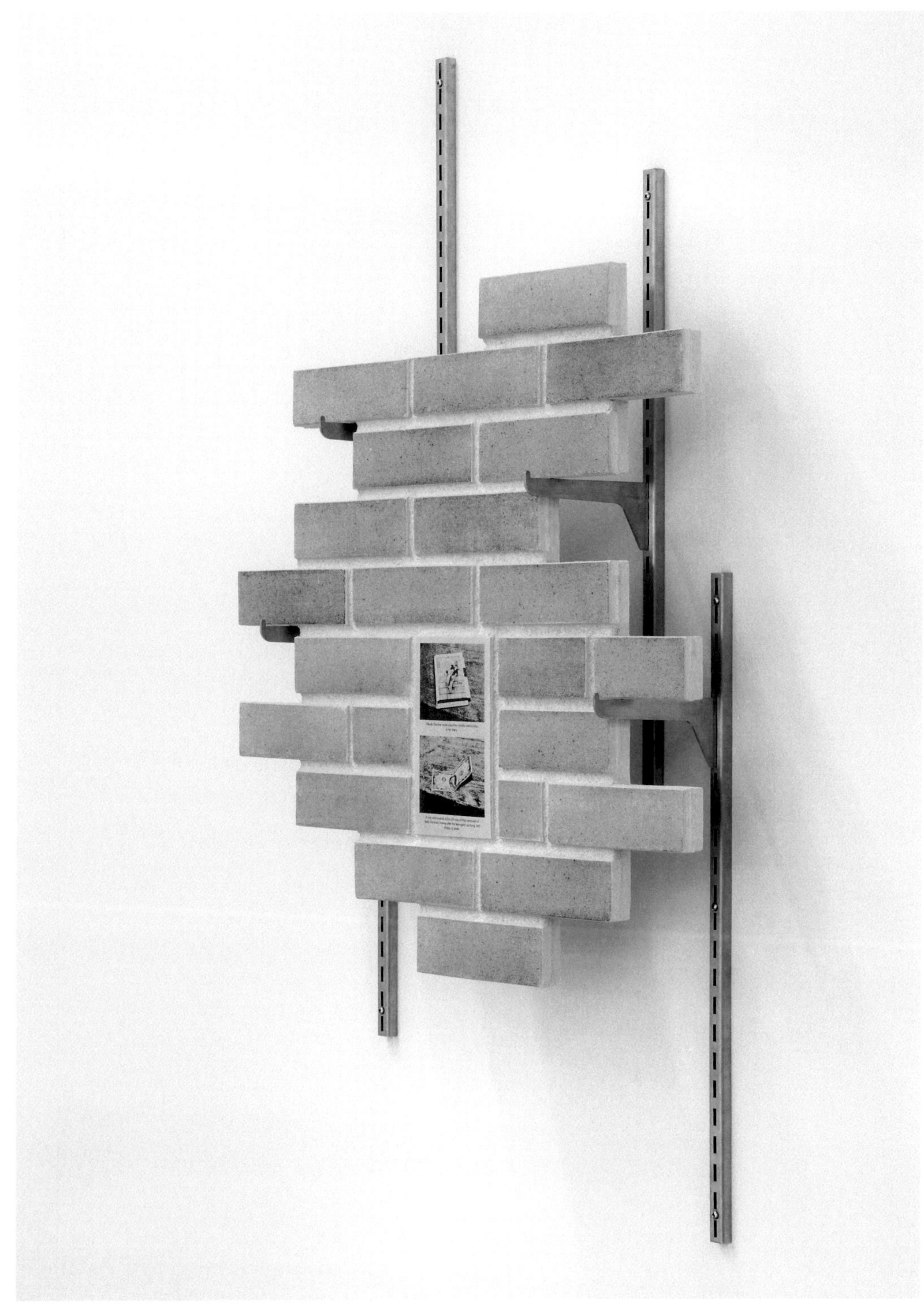

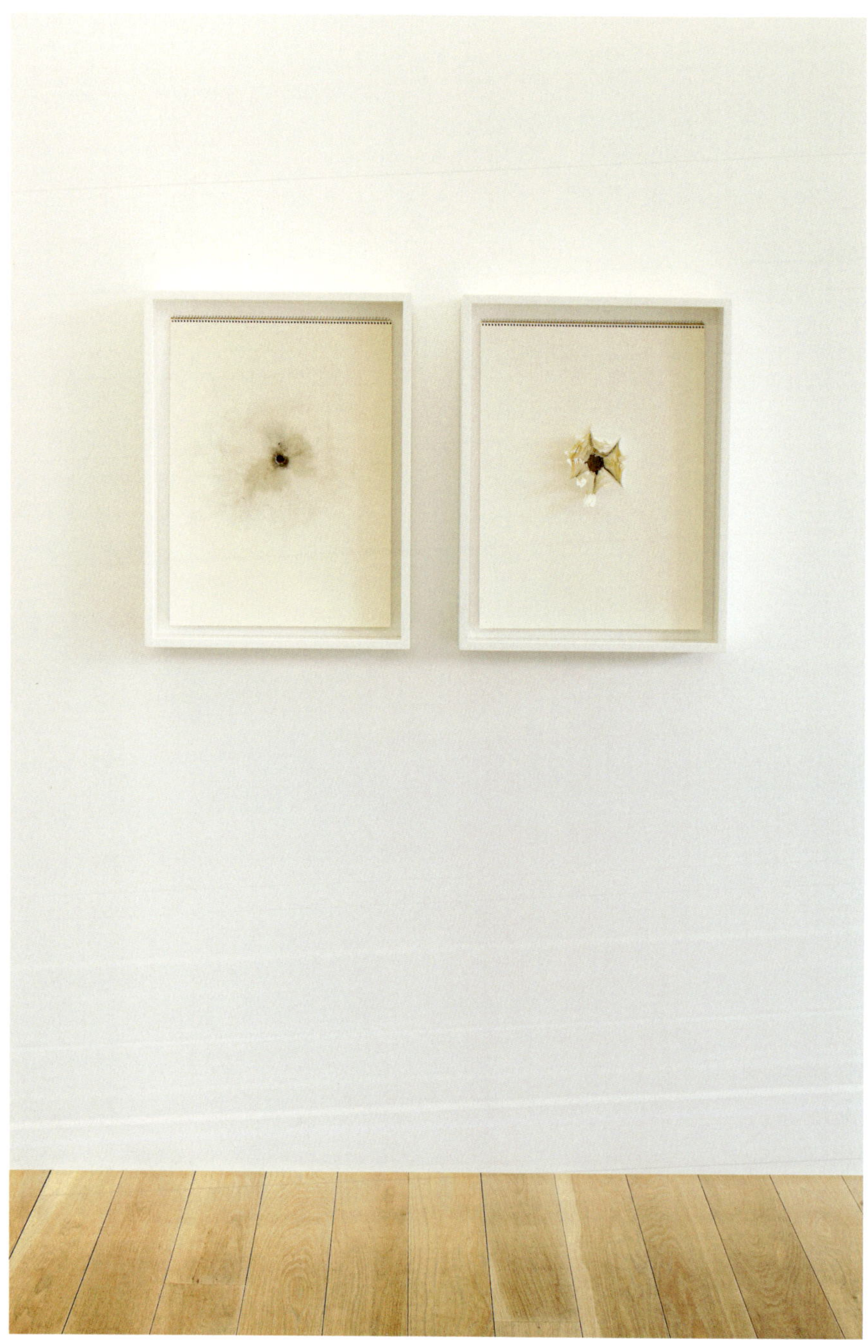

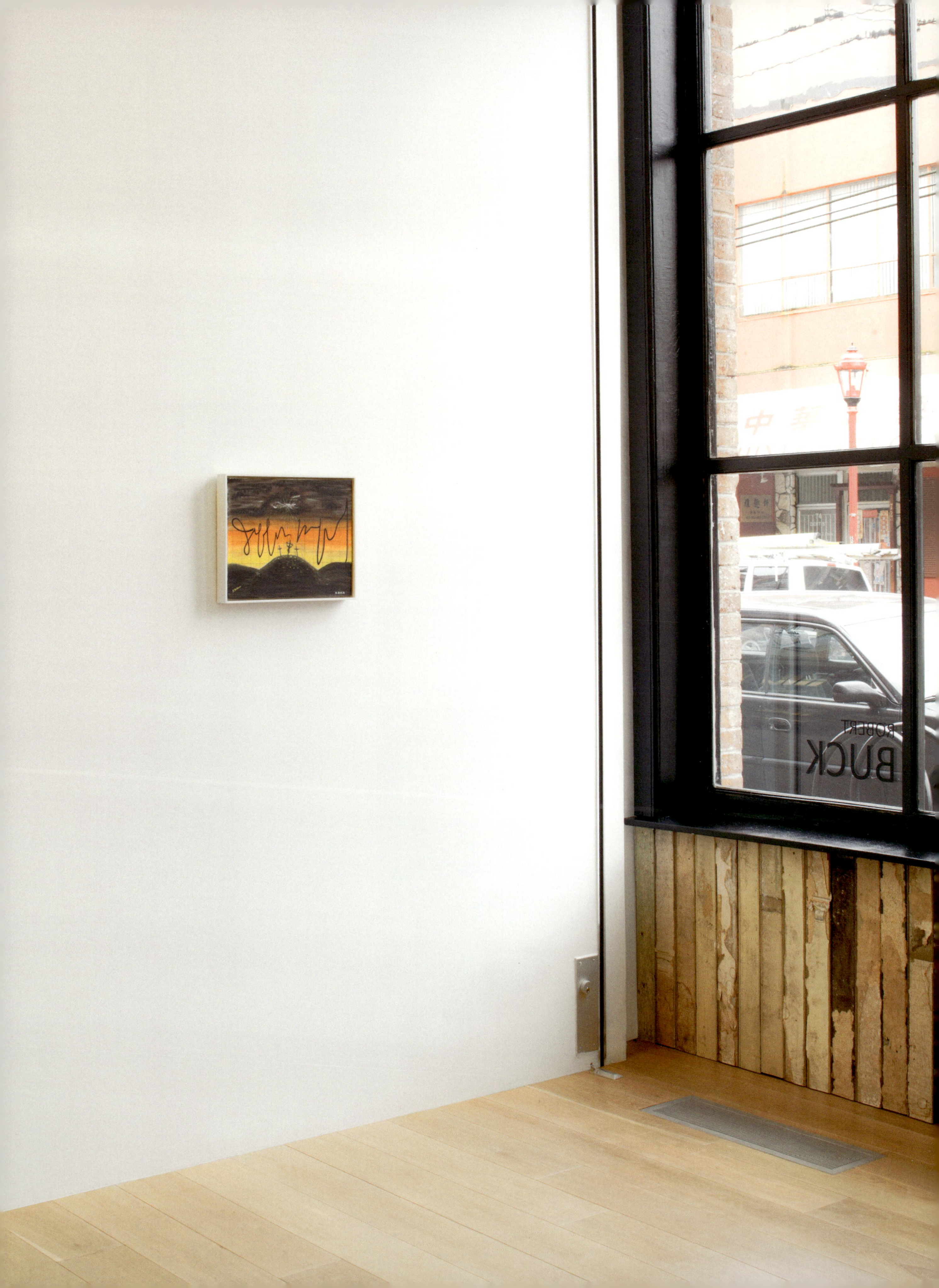

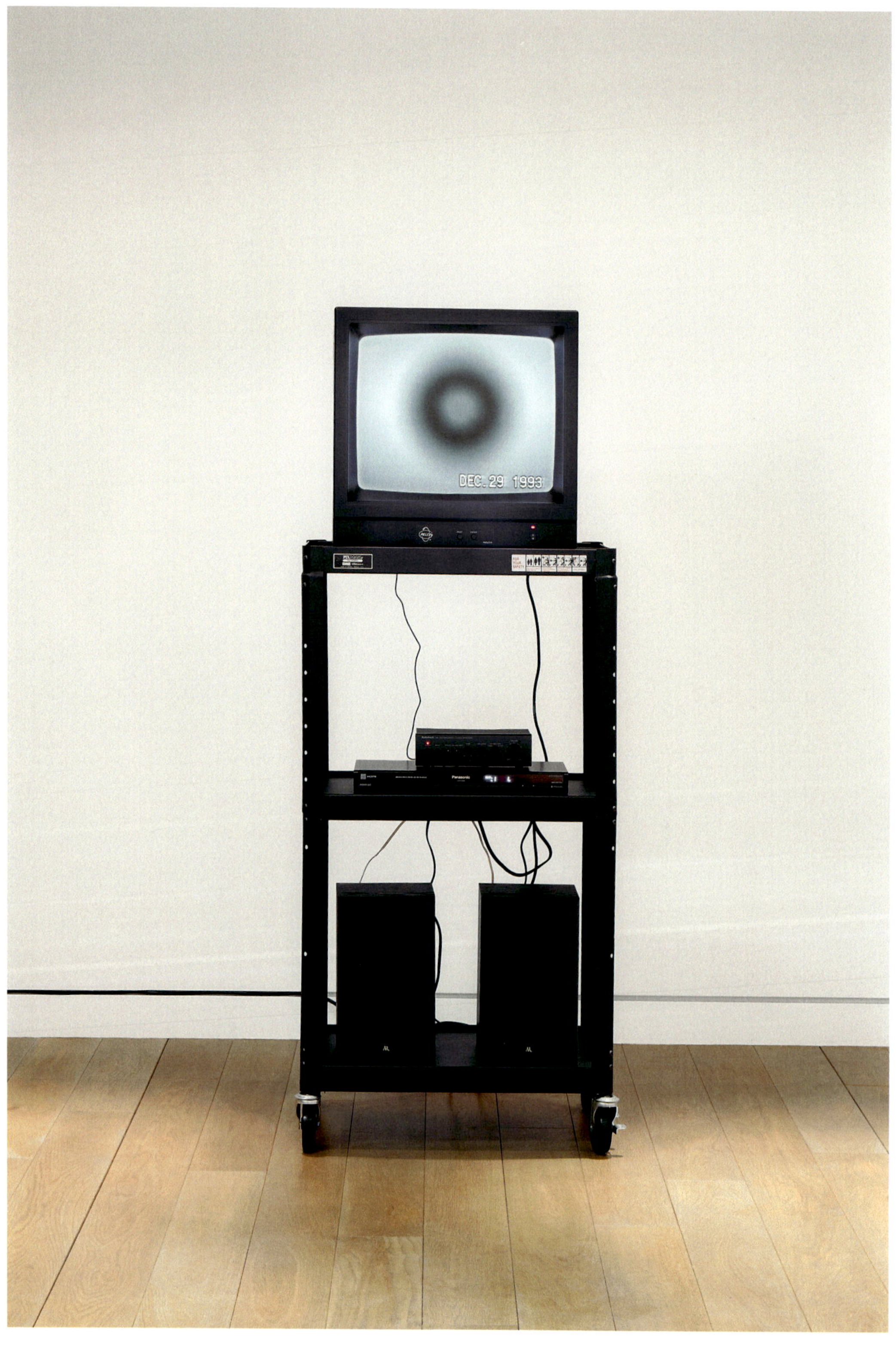

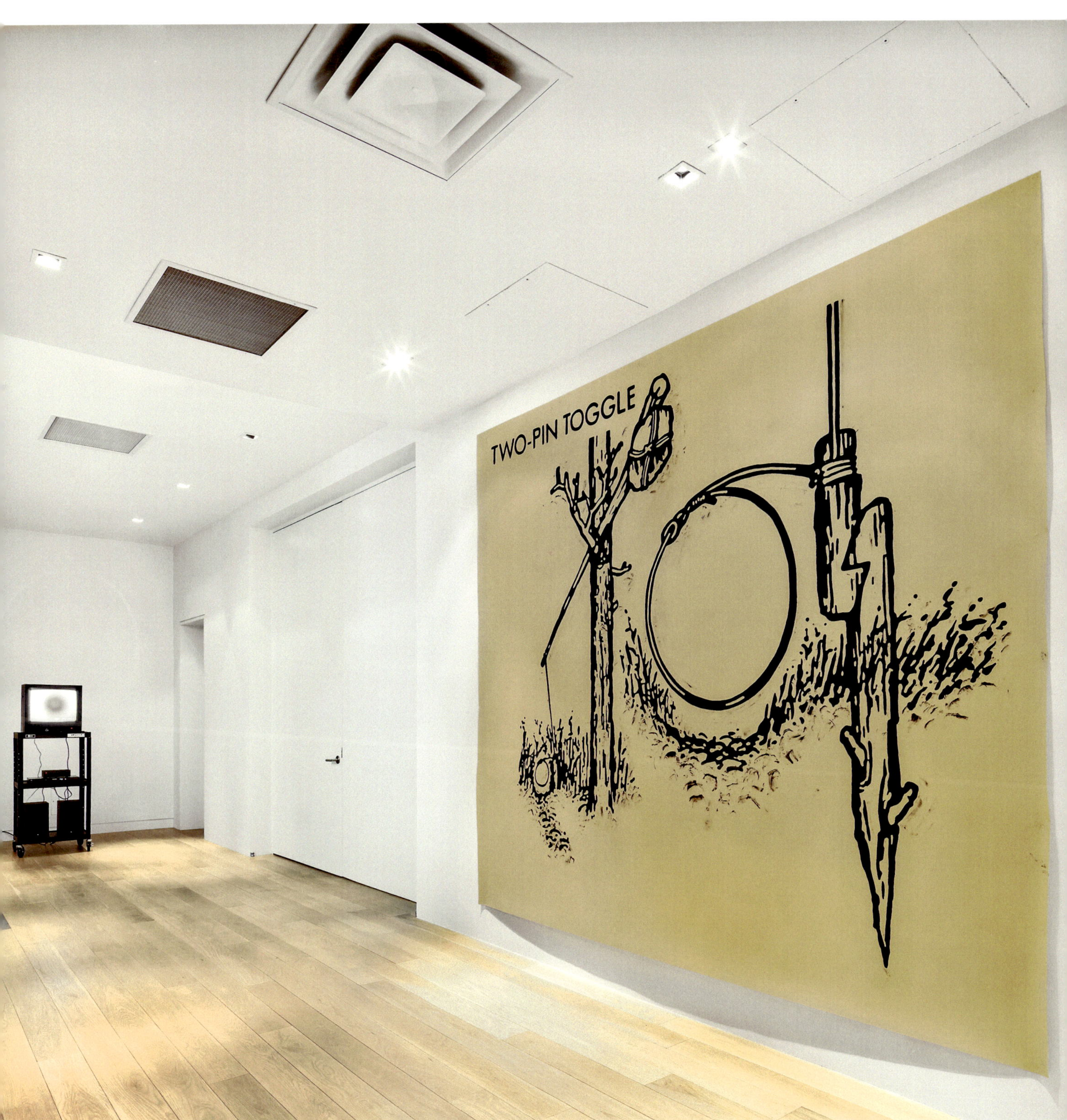
TWO-PIN TOGGLE

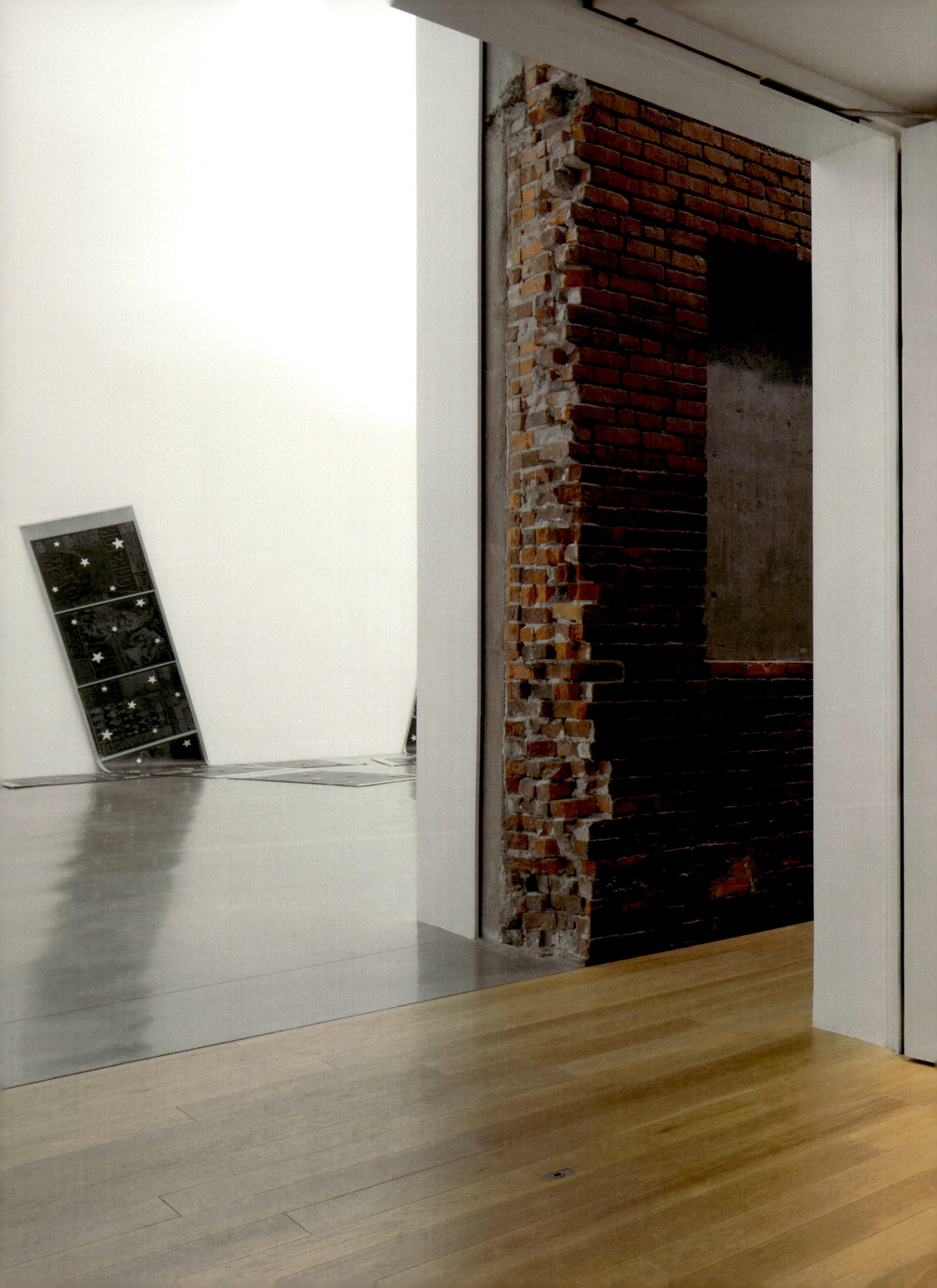

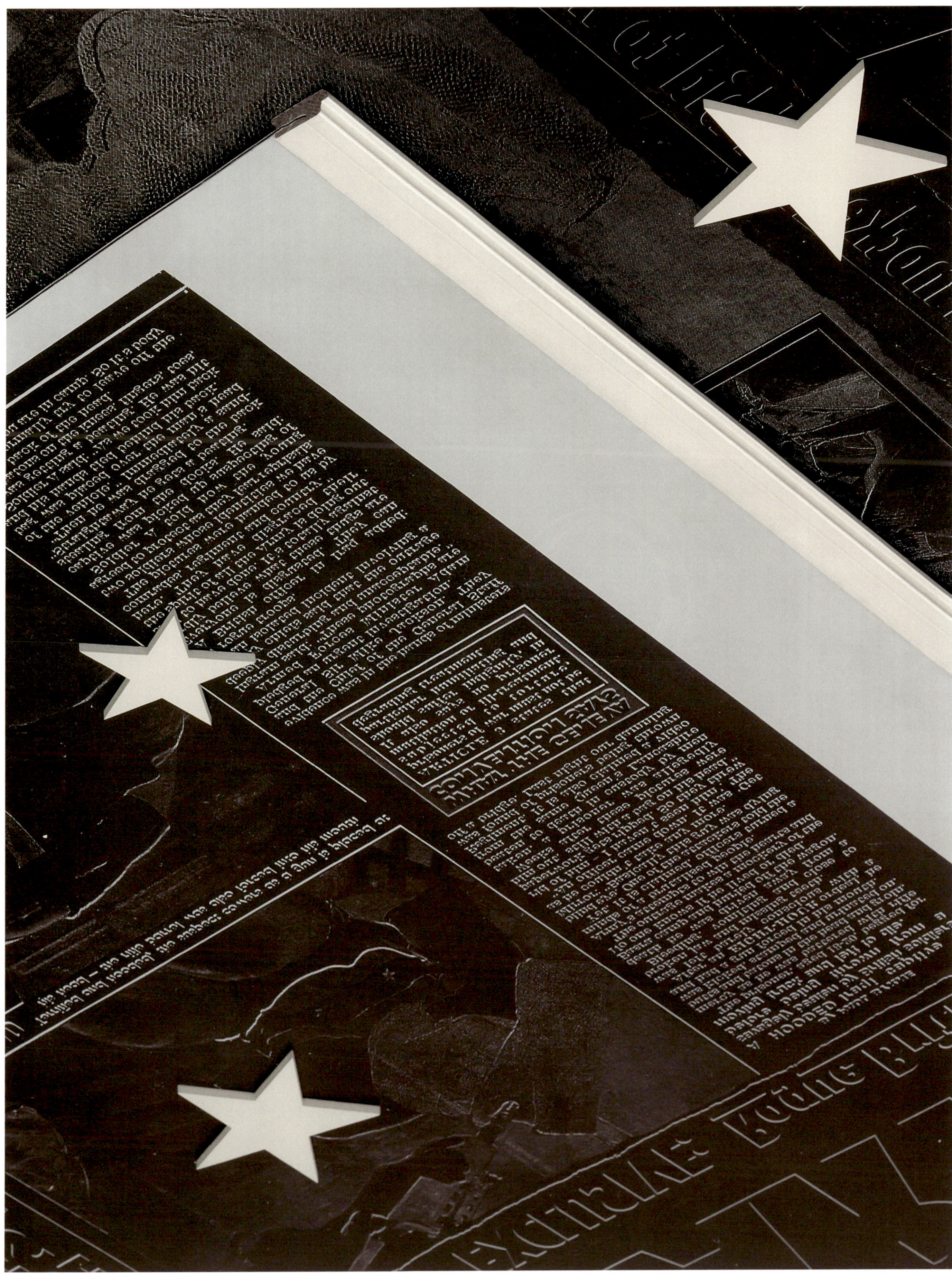

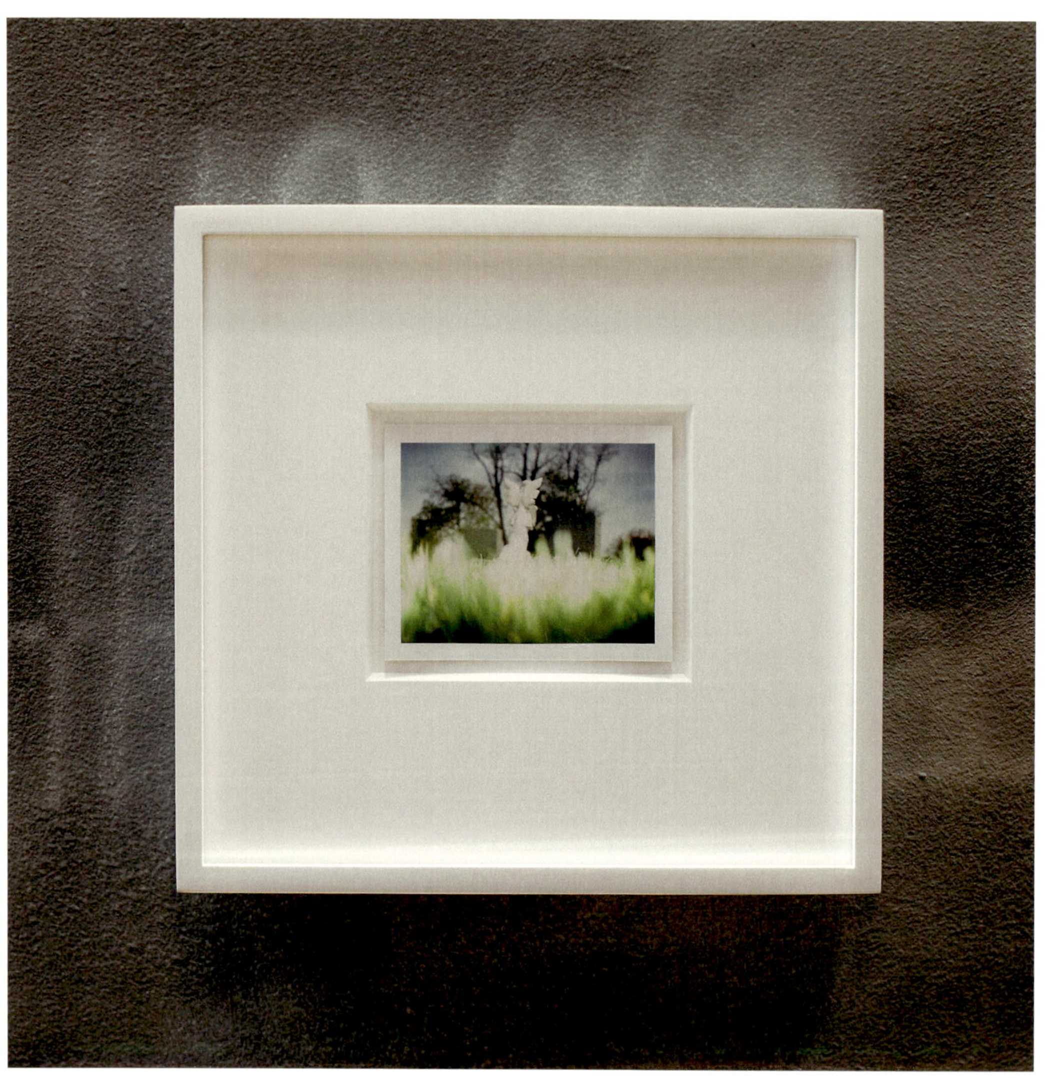

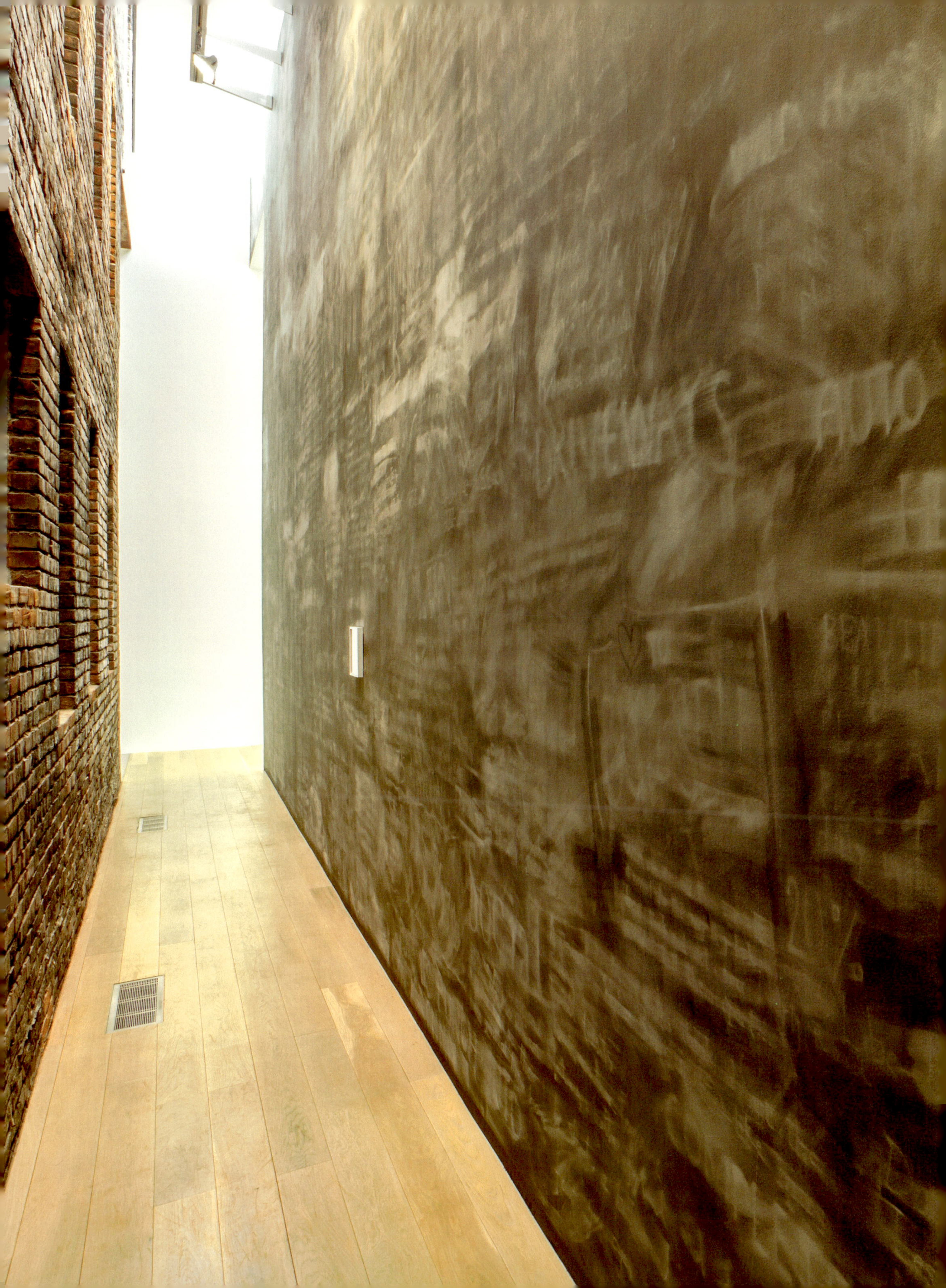

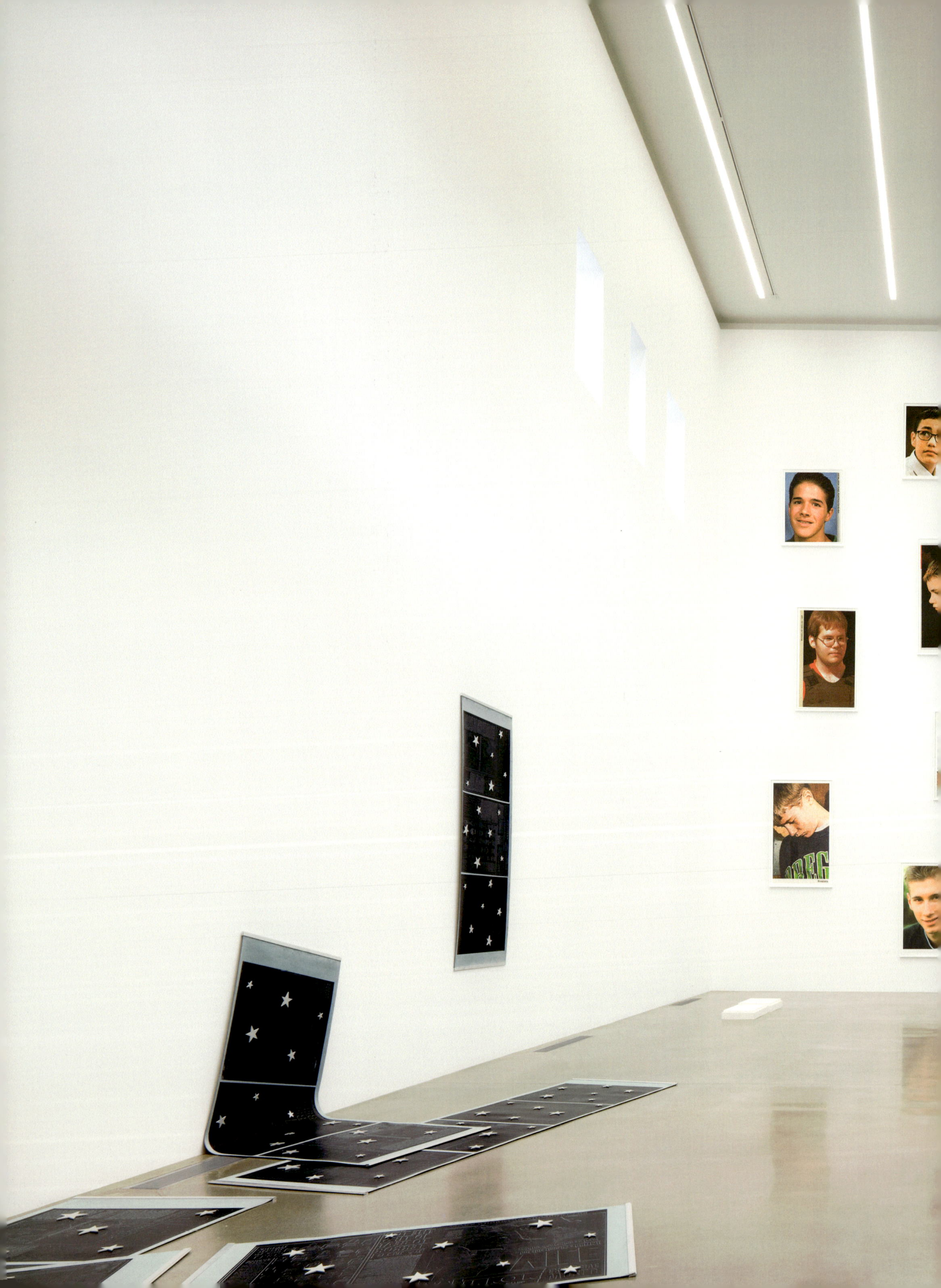

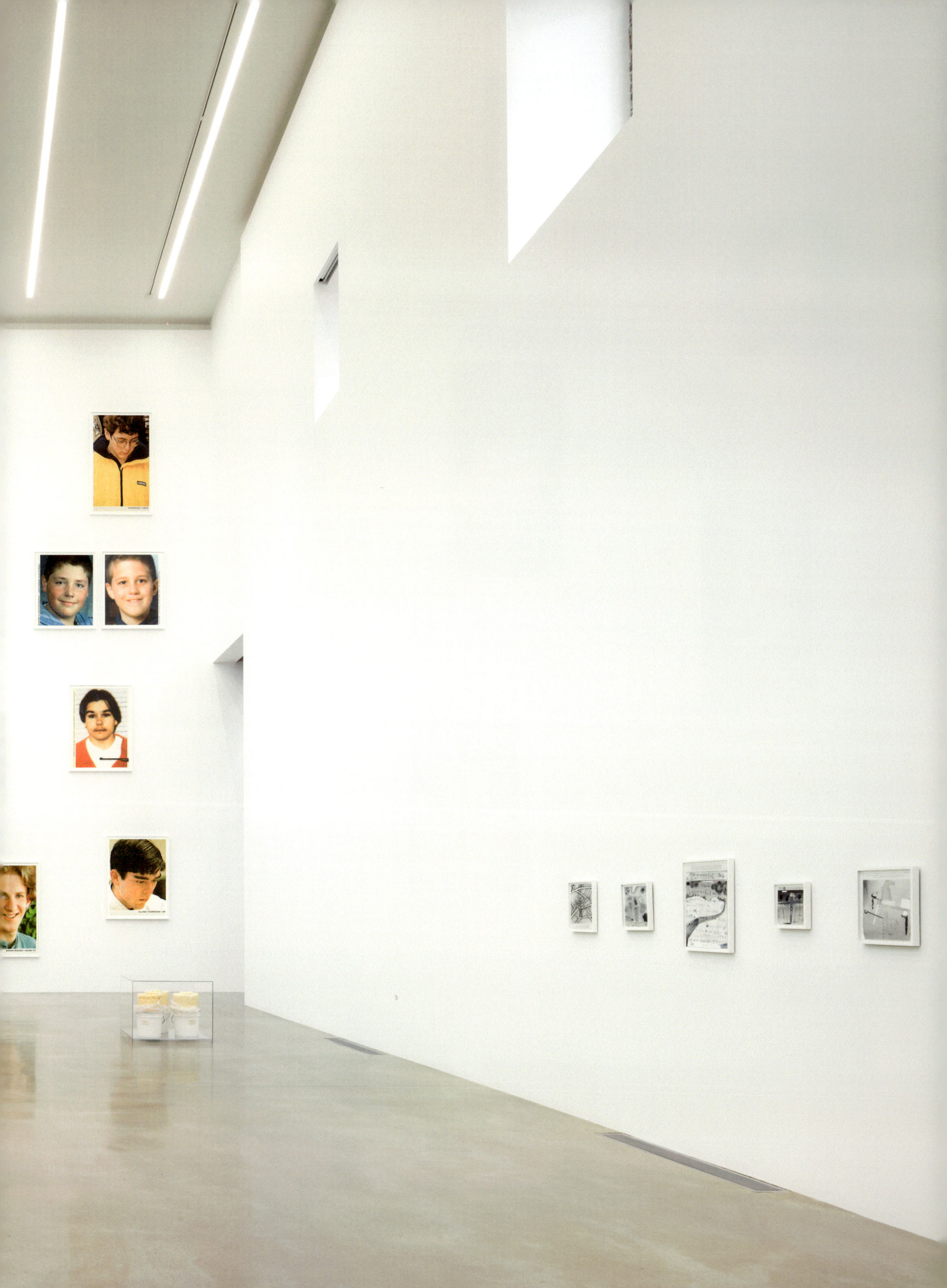

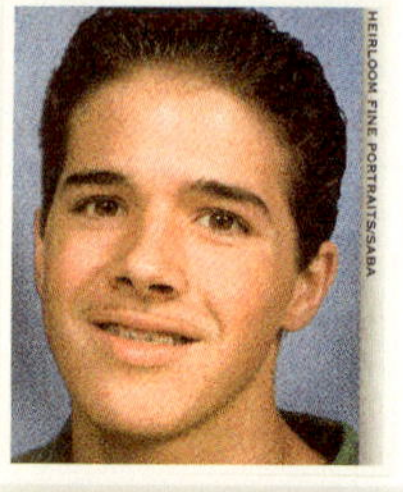

HEIRLOOM FINE PORTRAITS/SABA

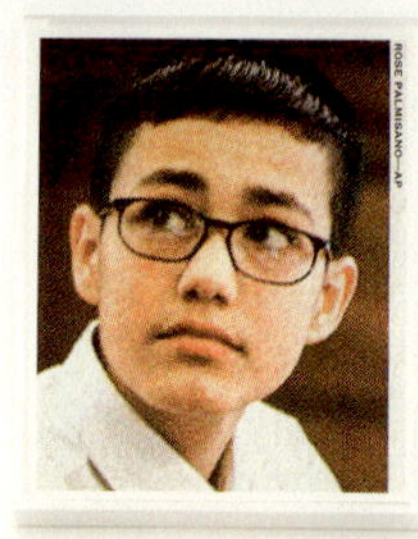

ROSIE PALMISANO—AP

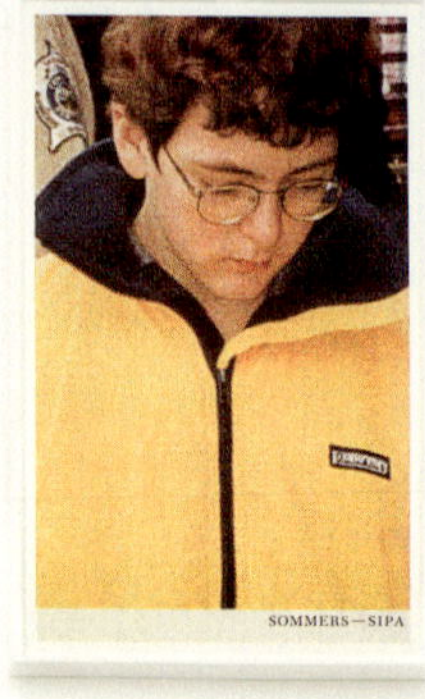

SOMMERS—SIPA

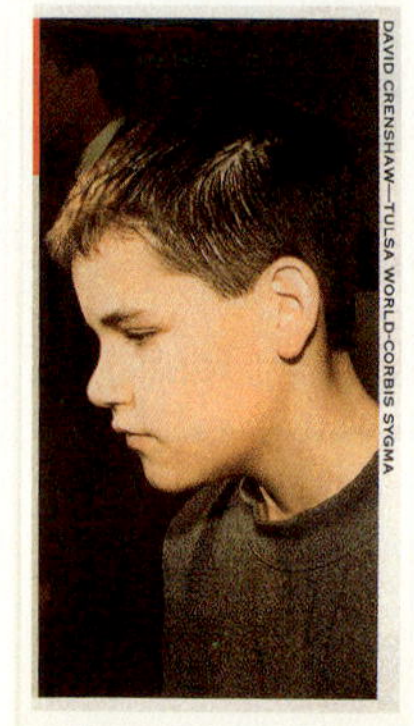

DAVID CRENSHAW—TULSA WORLD-CORBIS SYGMA

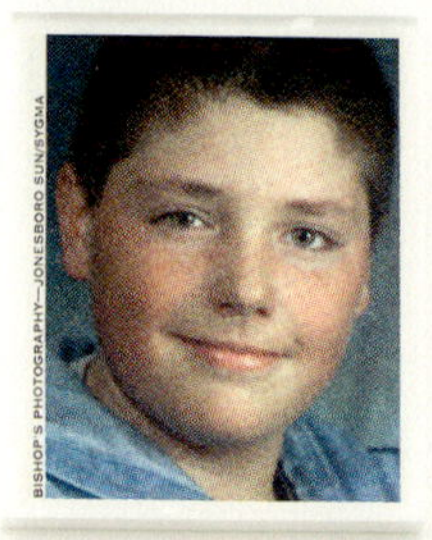
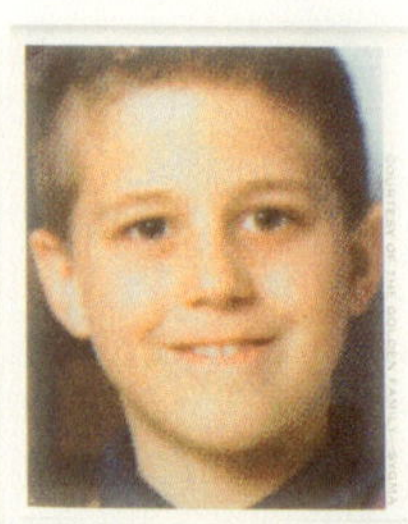

BISHOP'S PHOTOGRAPHY—JONESBORO SUN/SYGMA

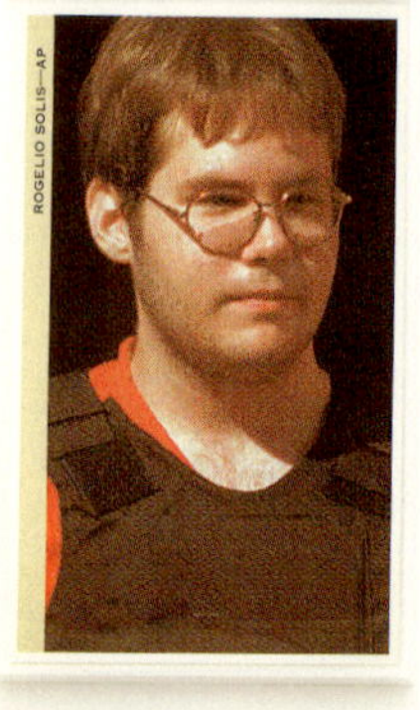

ROGELIO SOLIS—AP

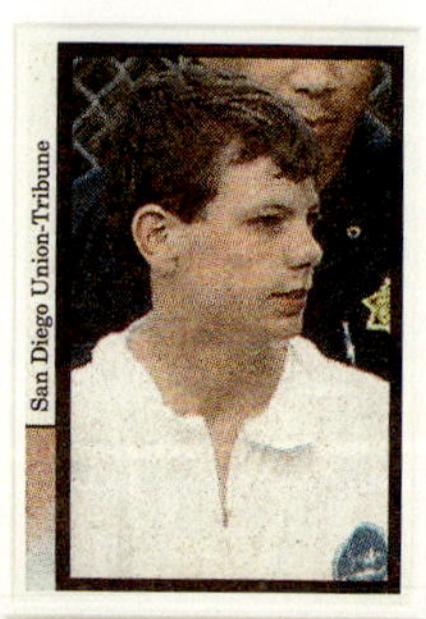

San Diego Union-Tribune

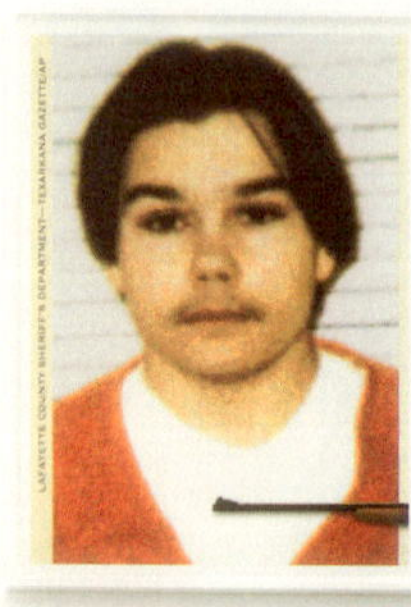

LANCASTER COUNTY SHERIFF'S DEPARTMENT—TUSKAHOMA GAZETTE/AP

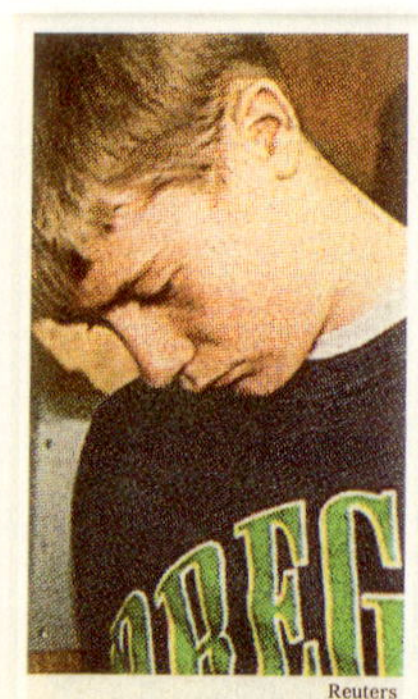

Reuters

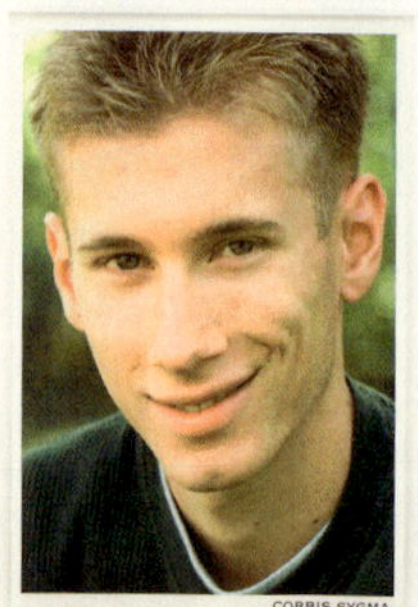

CORBIS SYGMA

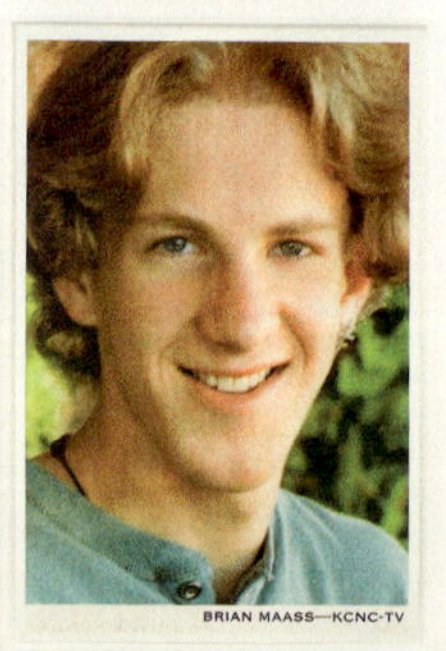

BRIAN MAASS—KCNC-TV

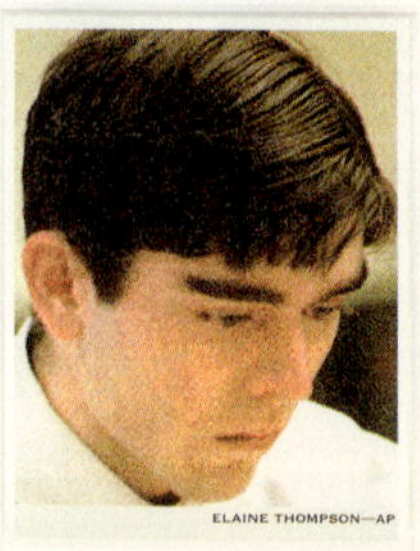

ELAINE THOMPSON—AP

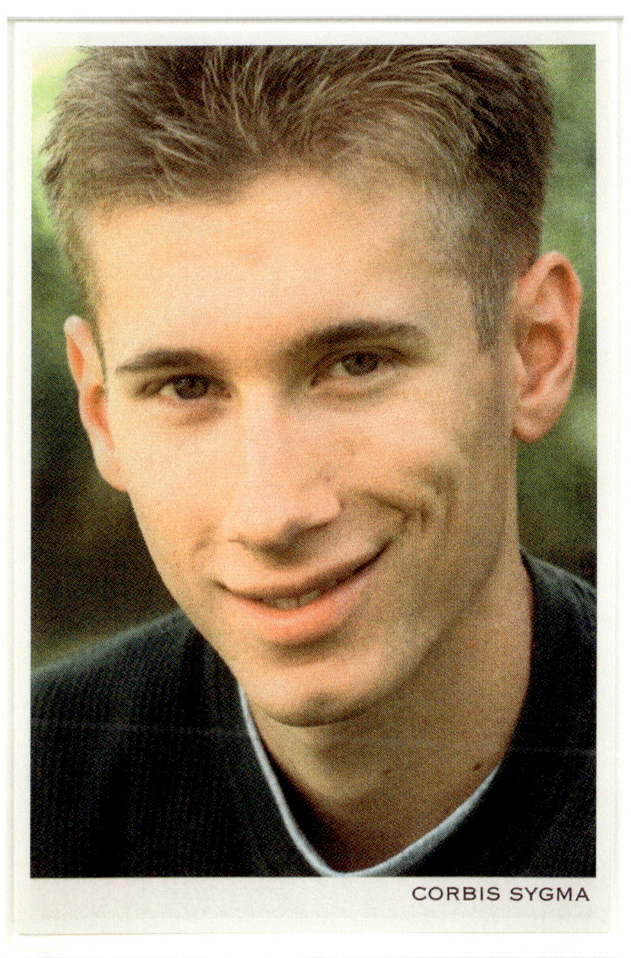

CORBIS SYGMA

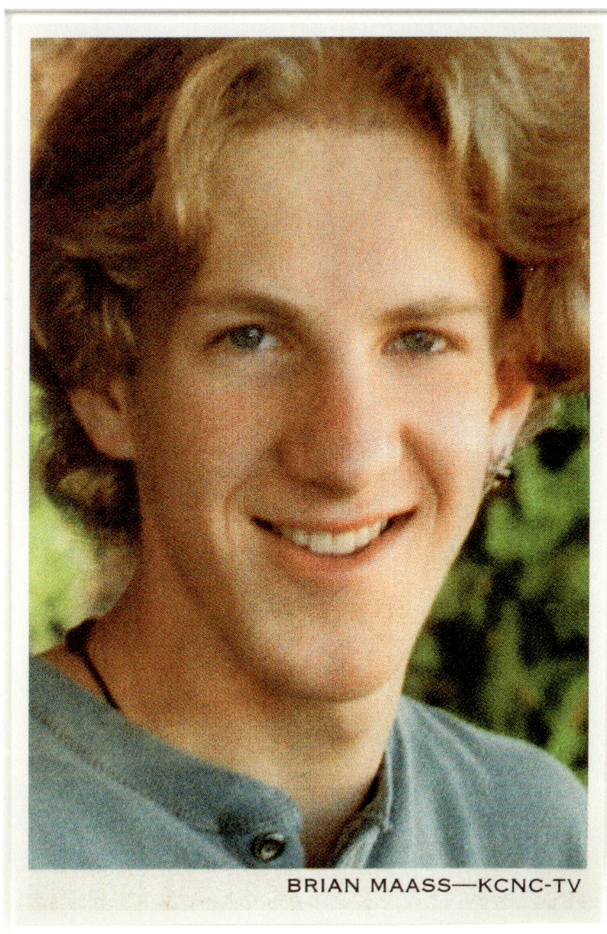

BRIAN MAASS—KCNC-TV

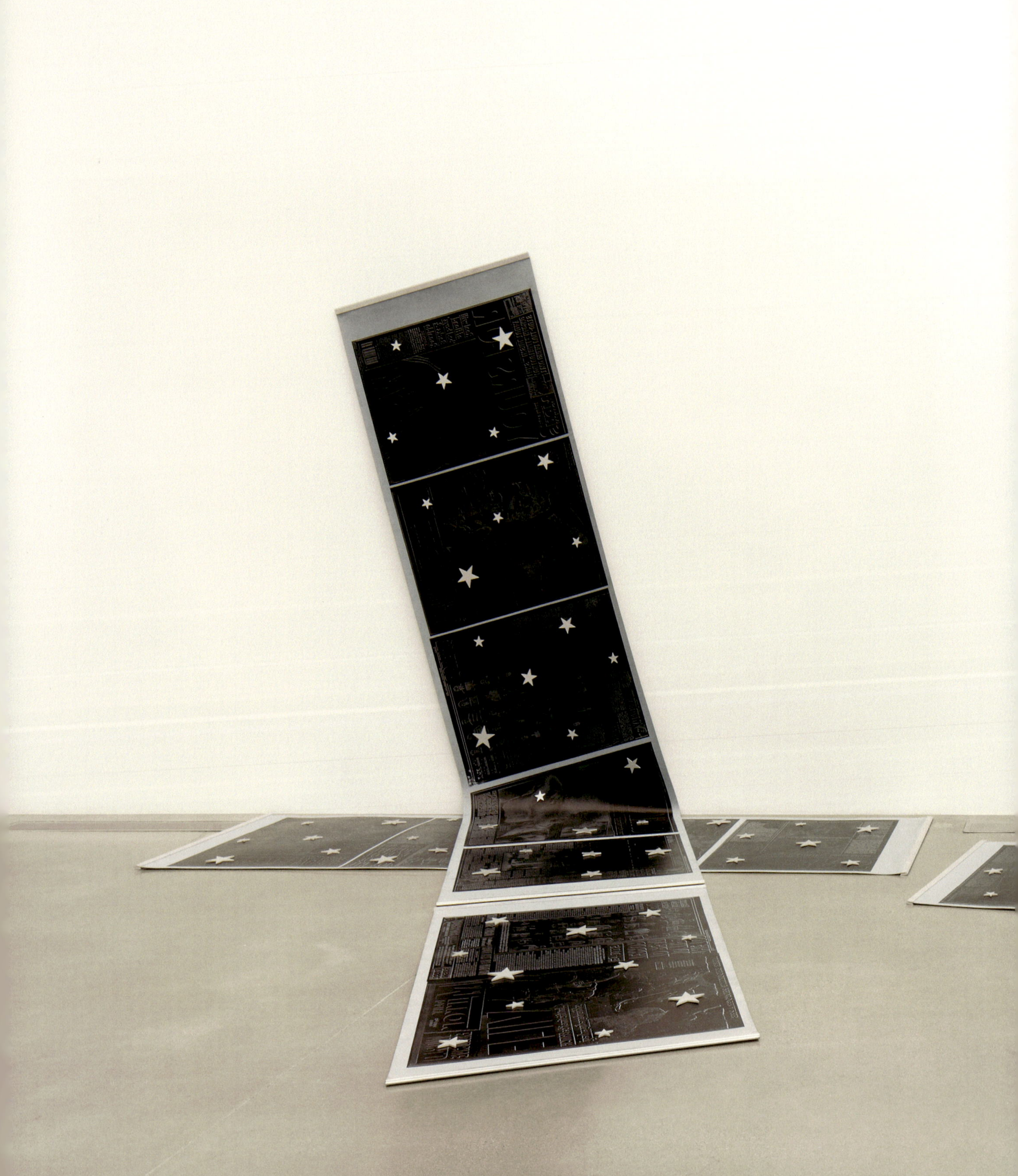

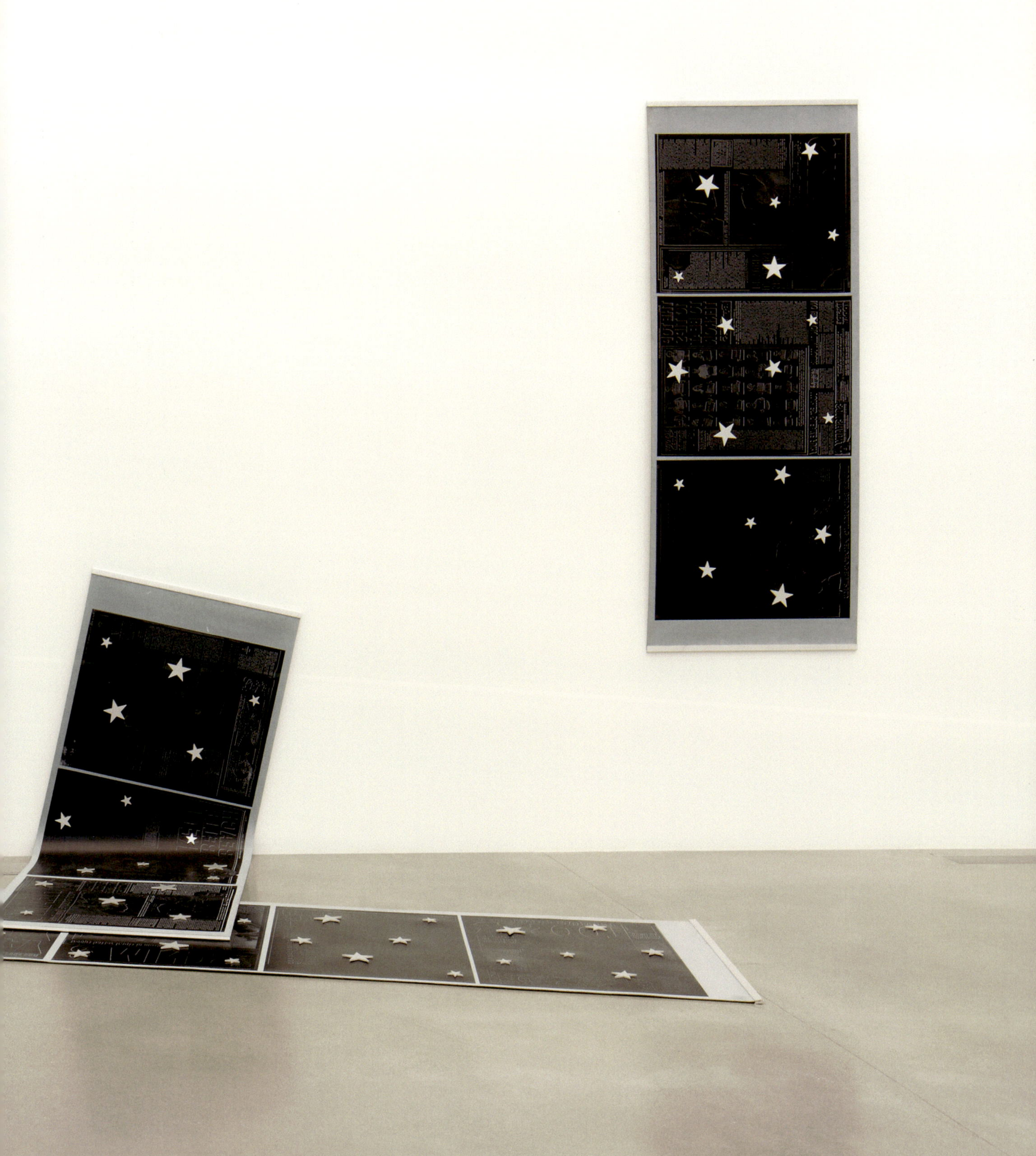

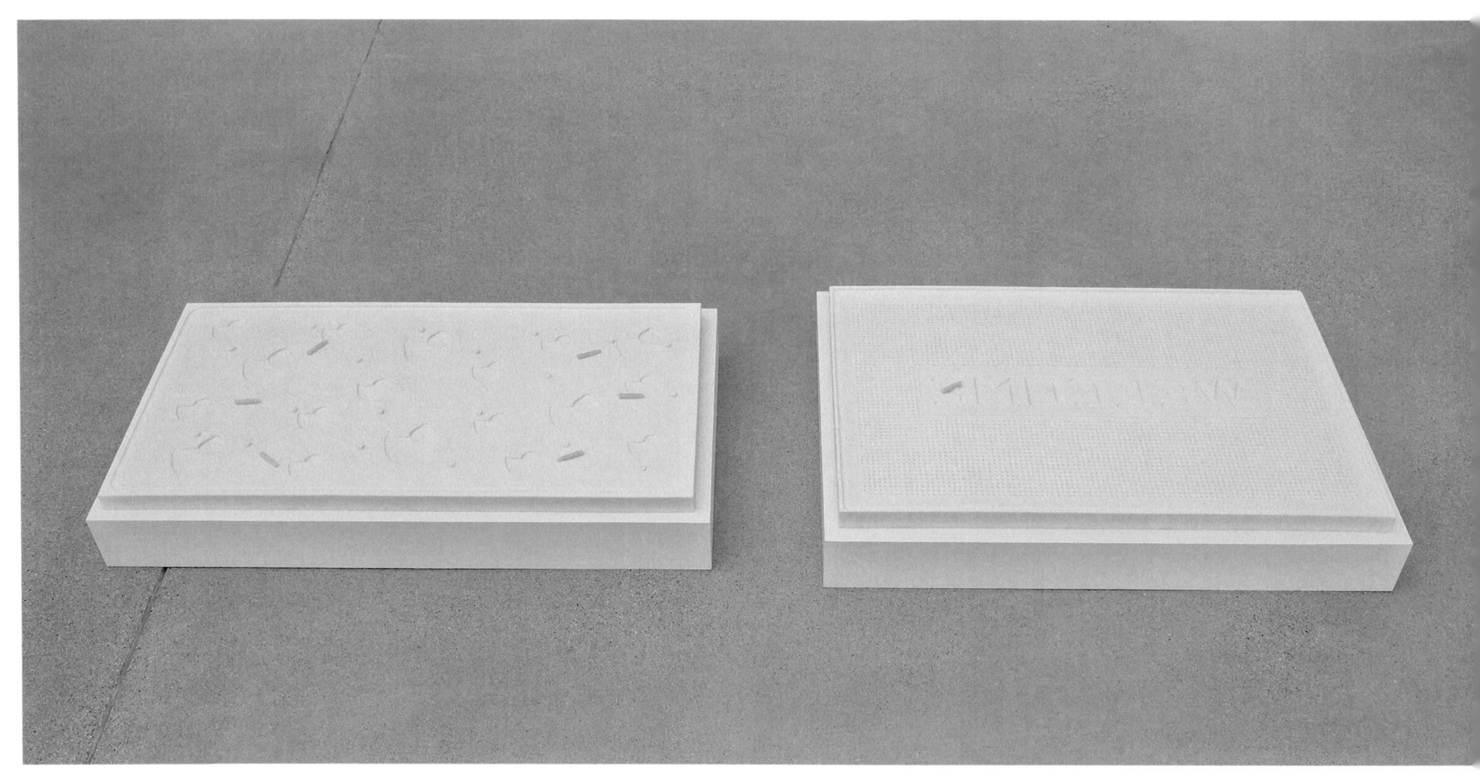

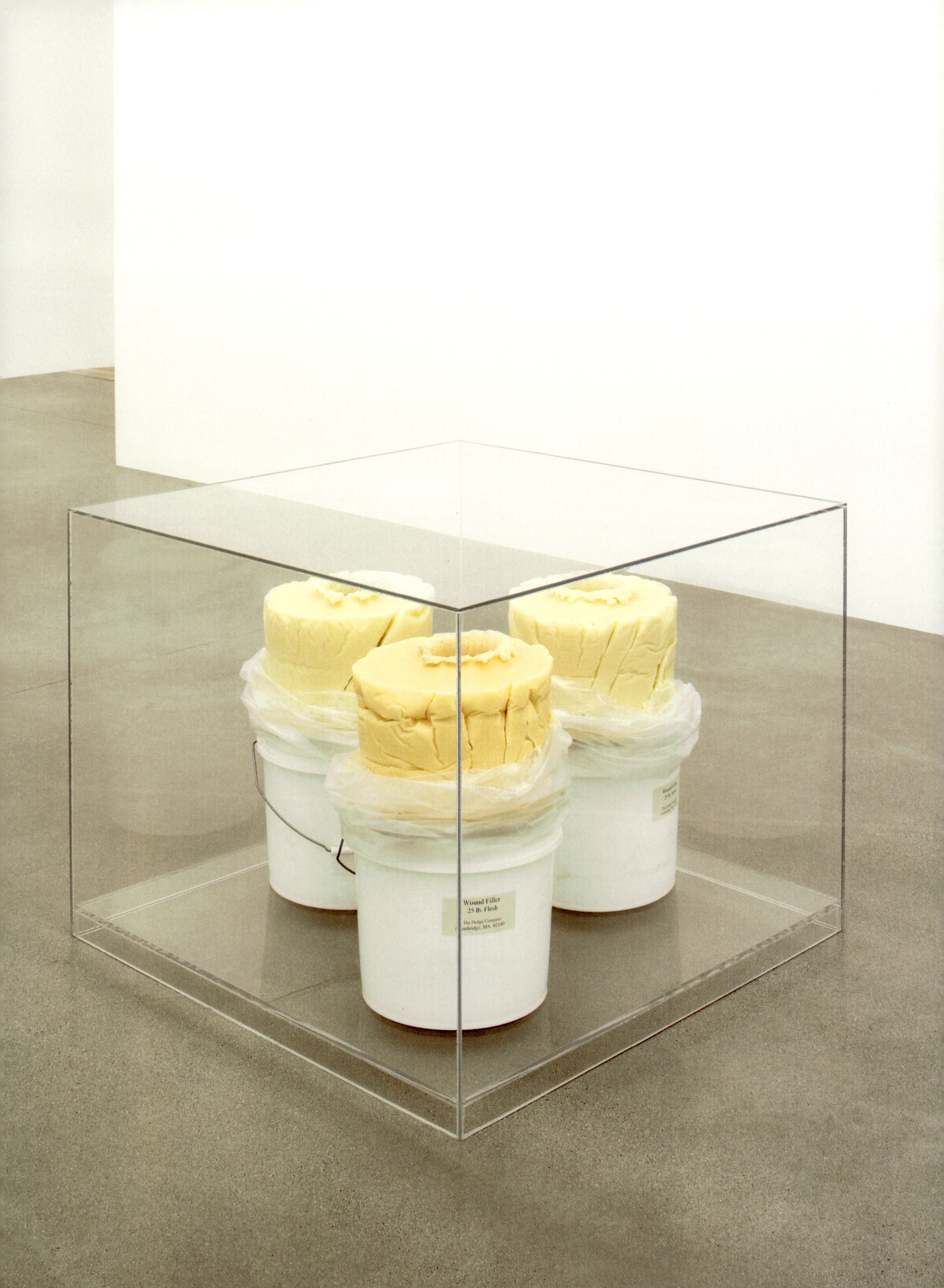

Wound Filler
25 lb. Flesh
The Dodge Company
Cambridge, MA 02140

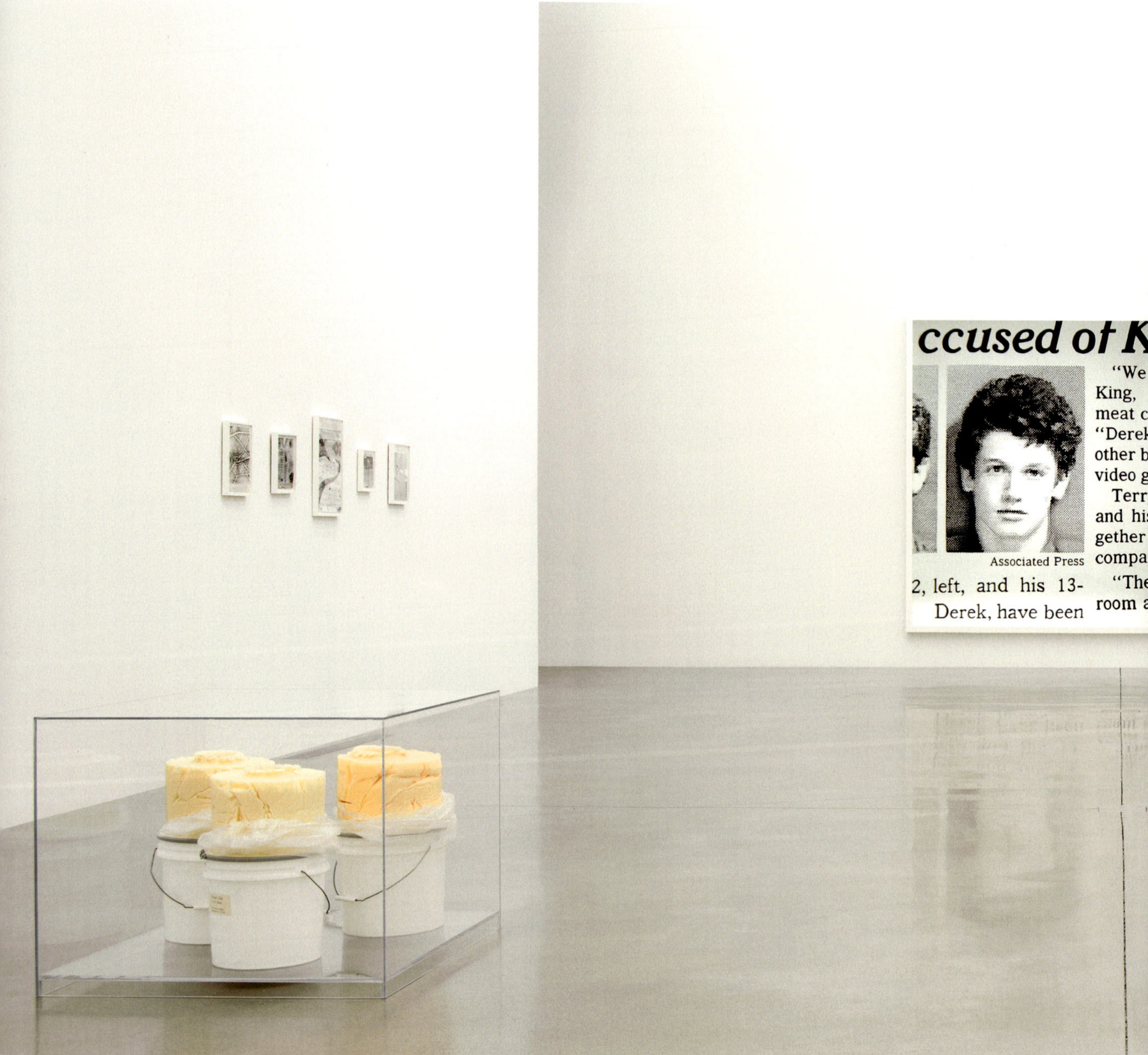
ccused of K
"We
King,
meat c
"Derek
other b
video g
Terr
and his
gether
compa
Associated Press
"The
2, left, and his 13-
room a
Derek, have been

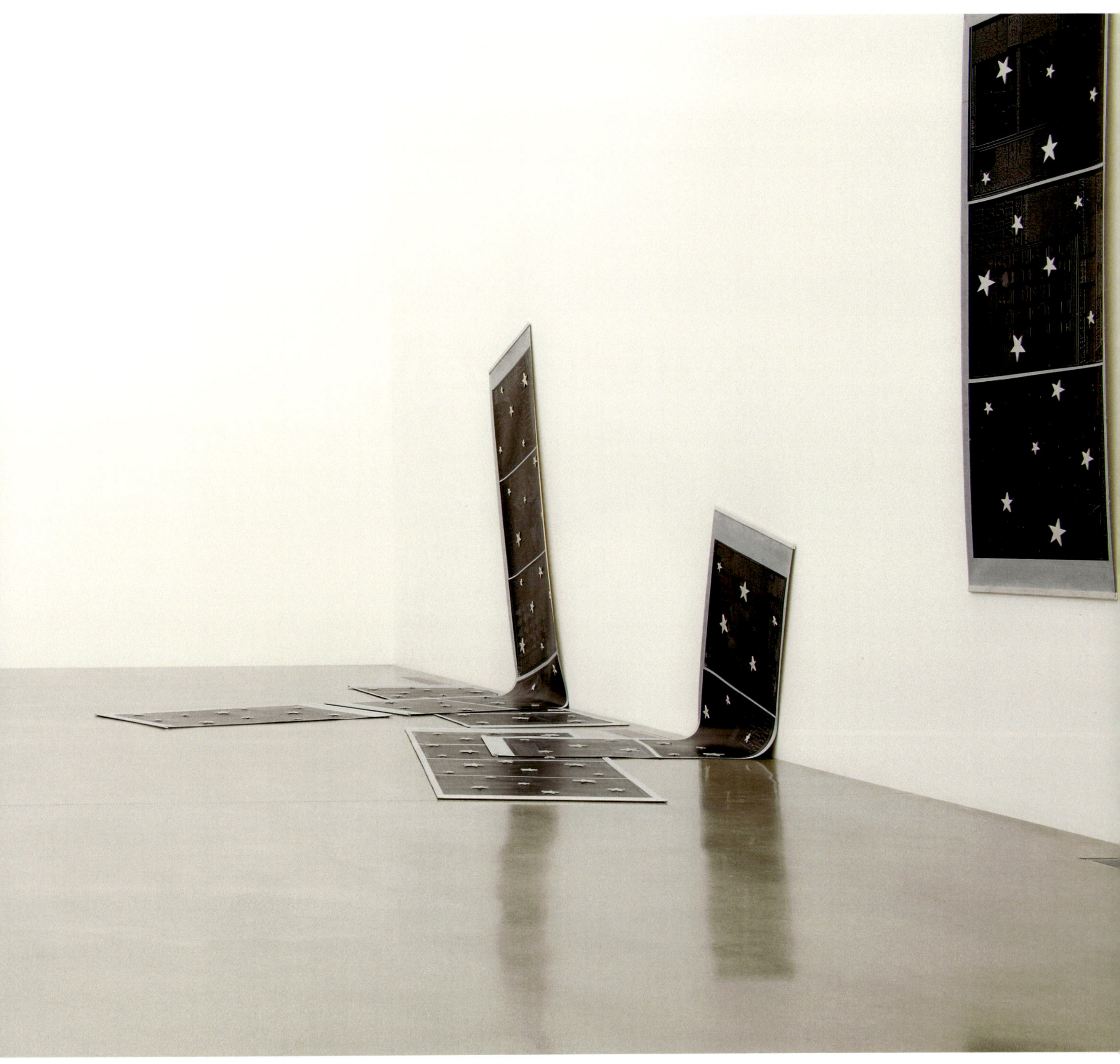

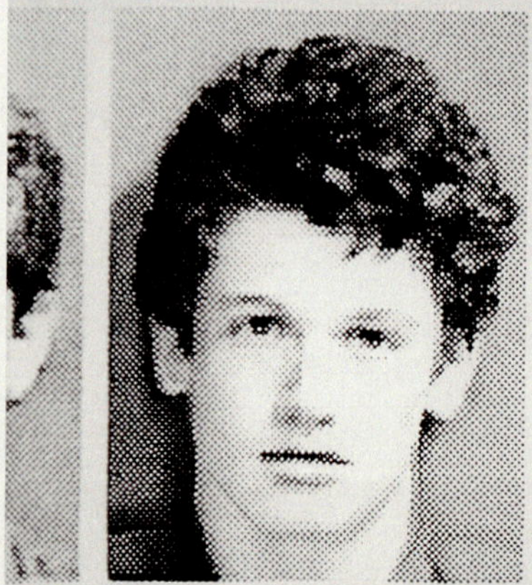
ccused of K
"We
King,
meat c
"Derek
other b
video g
Terry
and his
gether
Associated Press   compar
2, left, and his 13-   "The
Derek, have been   room a

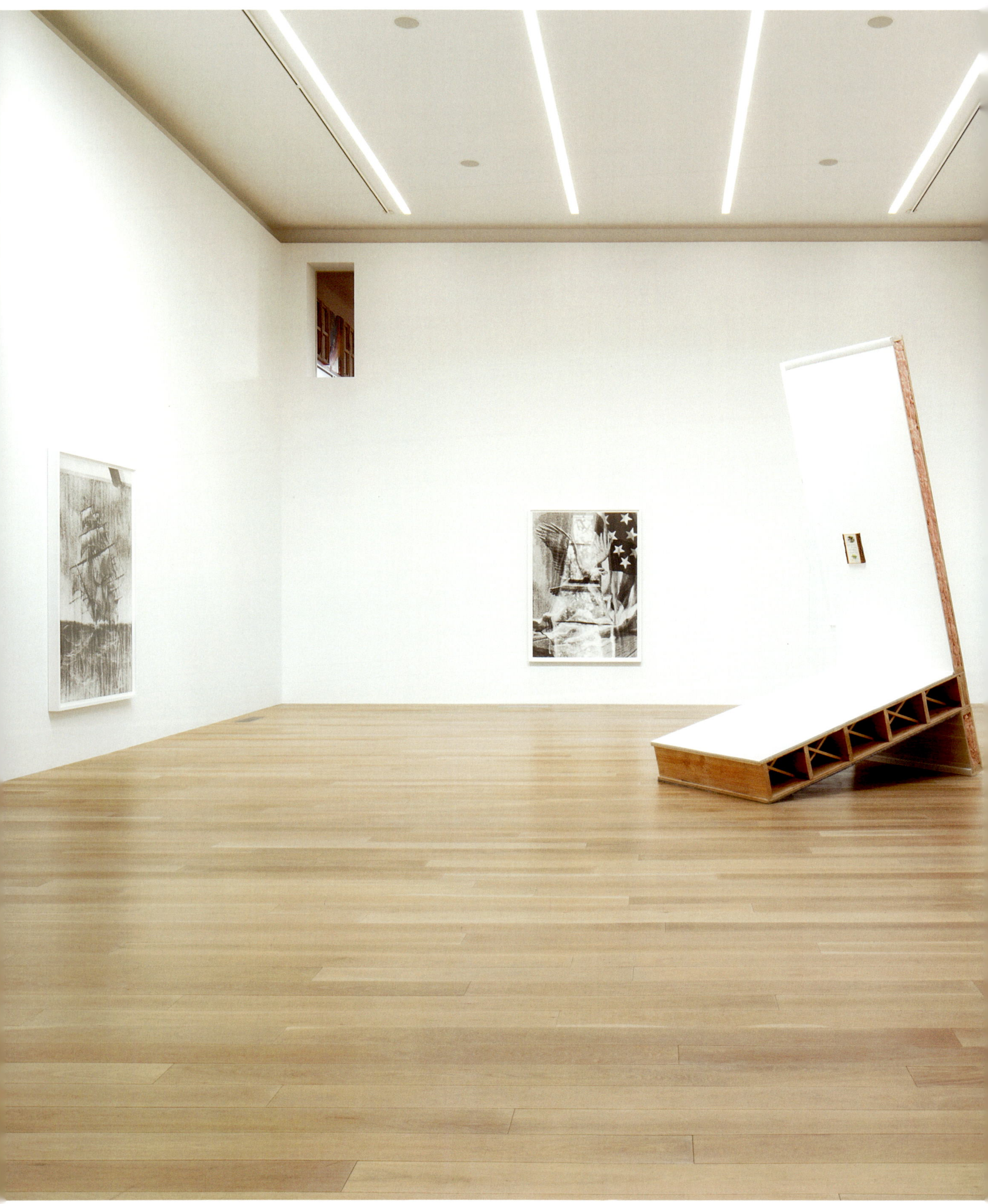

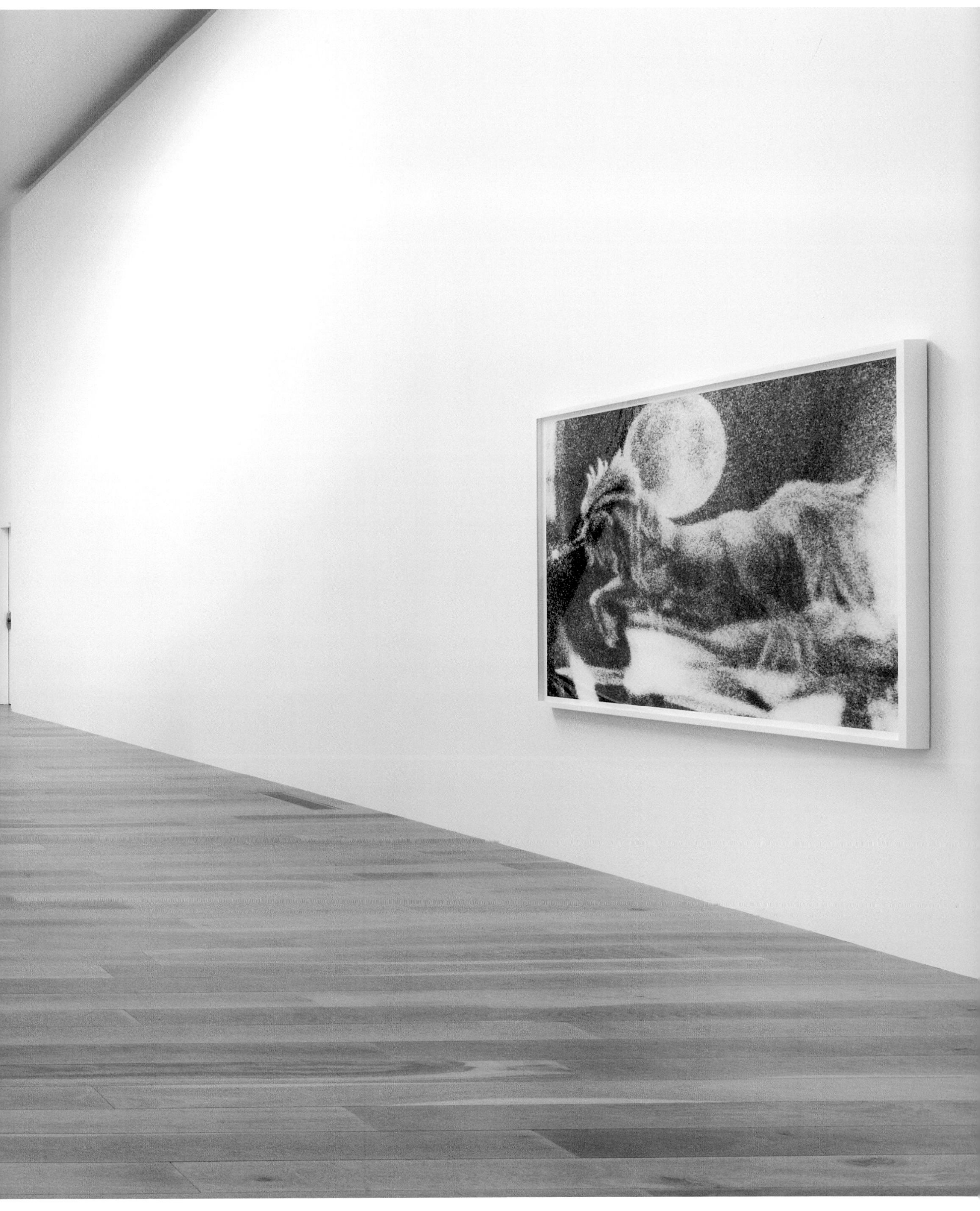

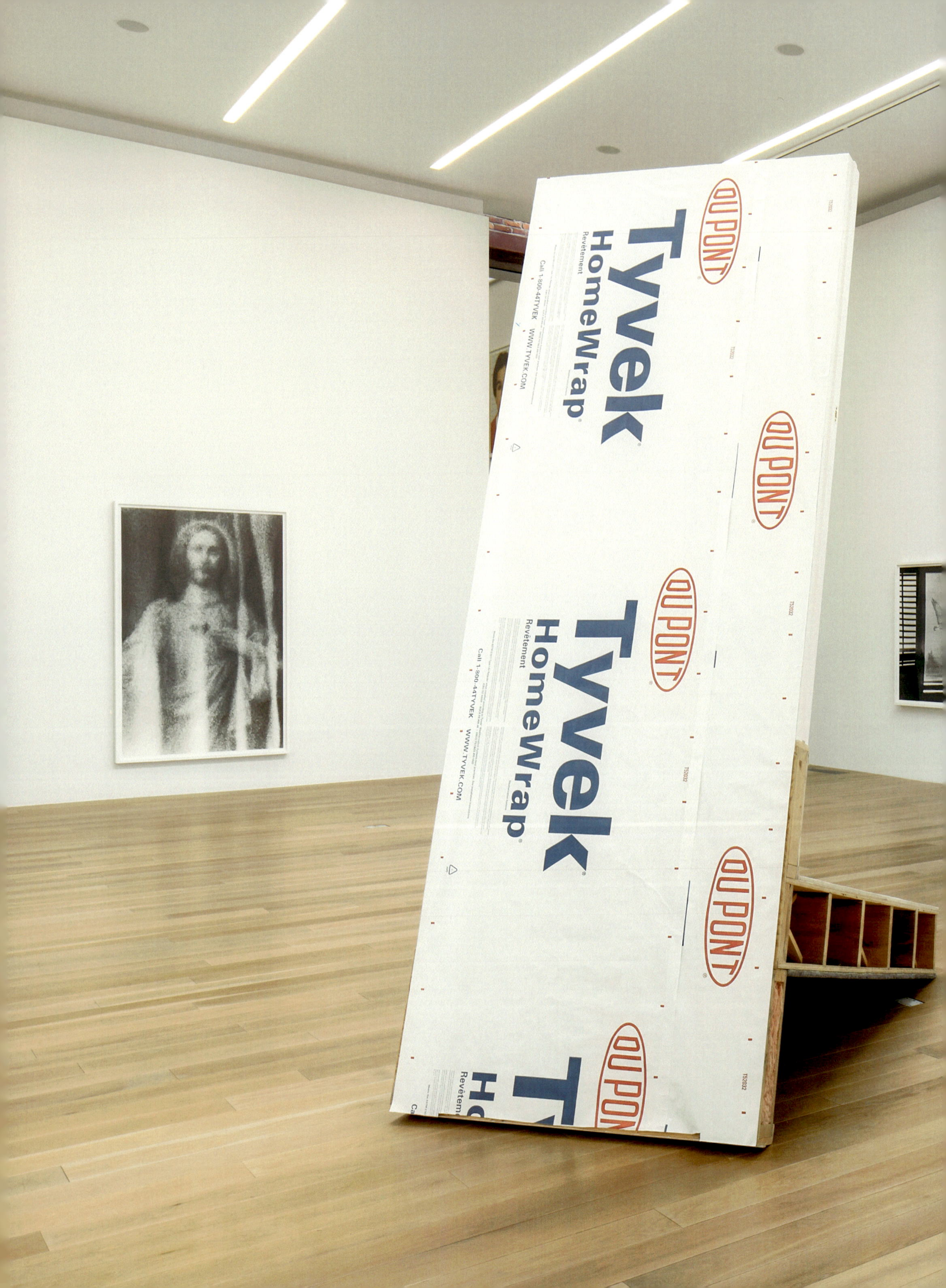
DU PONT
Tyvek
HomeWrap
Revêtement
Call 1-800-44TYVEK
WWW.TYVEK.COM

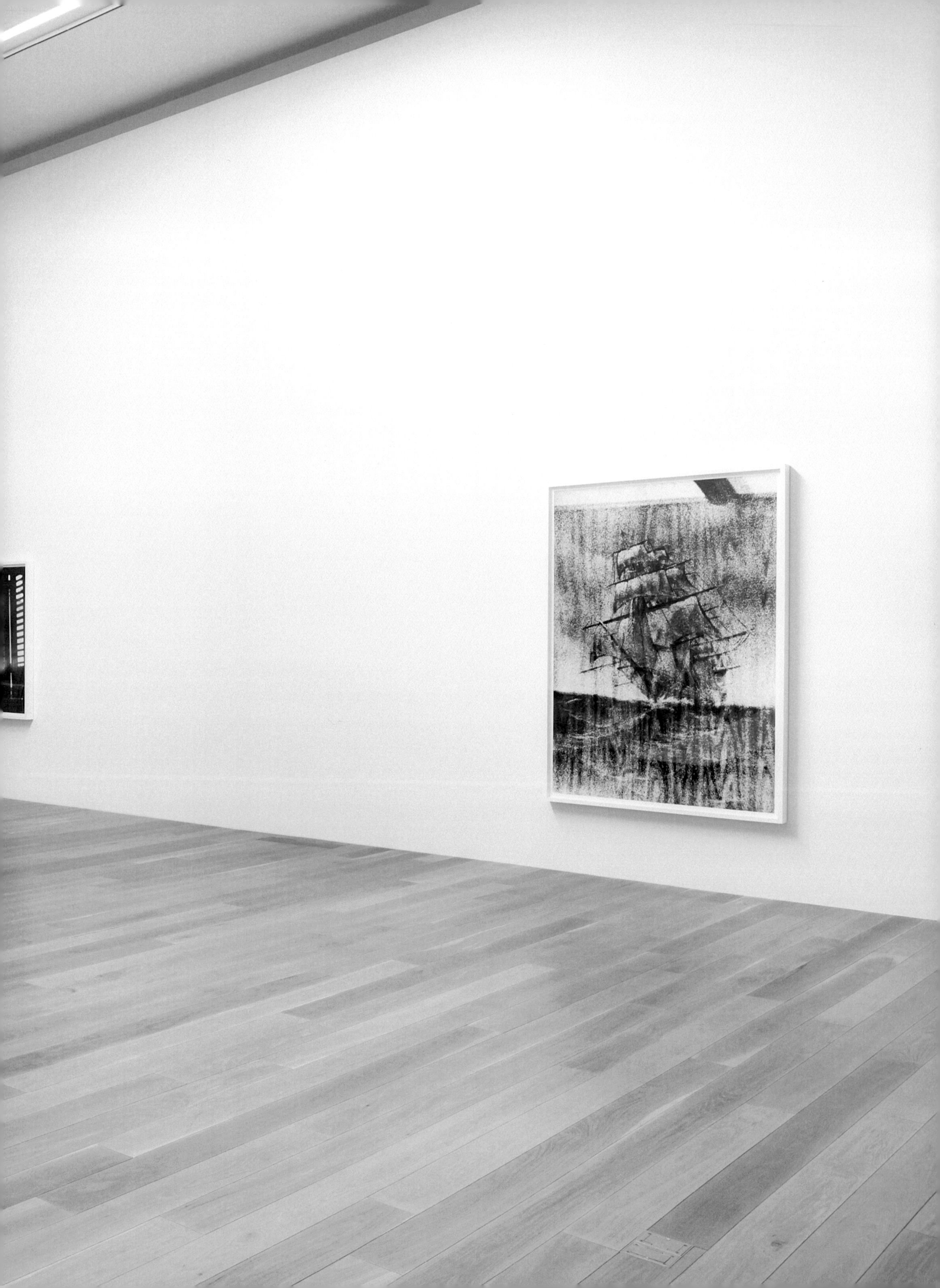

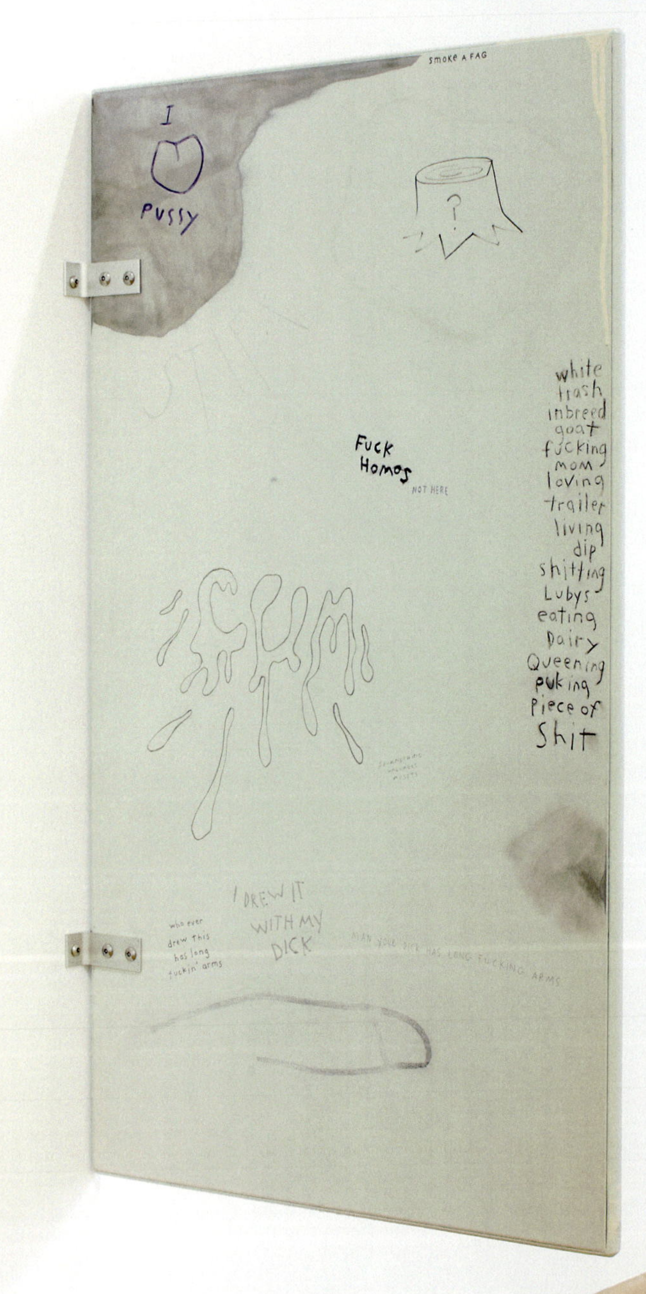

SMOKE A FAG
I ♥ PUSSY
?
FUCK HOMOS
NOT HERE
CUM
white
trash
inbreed
goat
fucking
mom
loving
trailer
living
dip
shitting
Lubys
eating
Dairy
Queening
puking
piece of
Shit
who ever
drew this
has long
fuckin' arms
I DREW IT
WITH MY
DICK

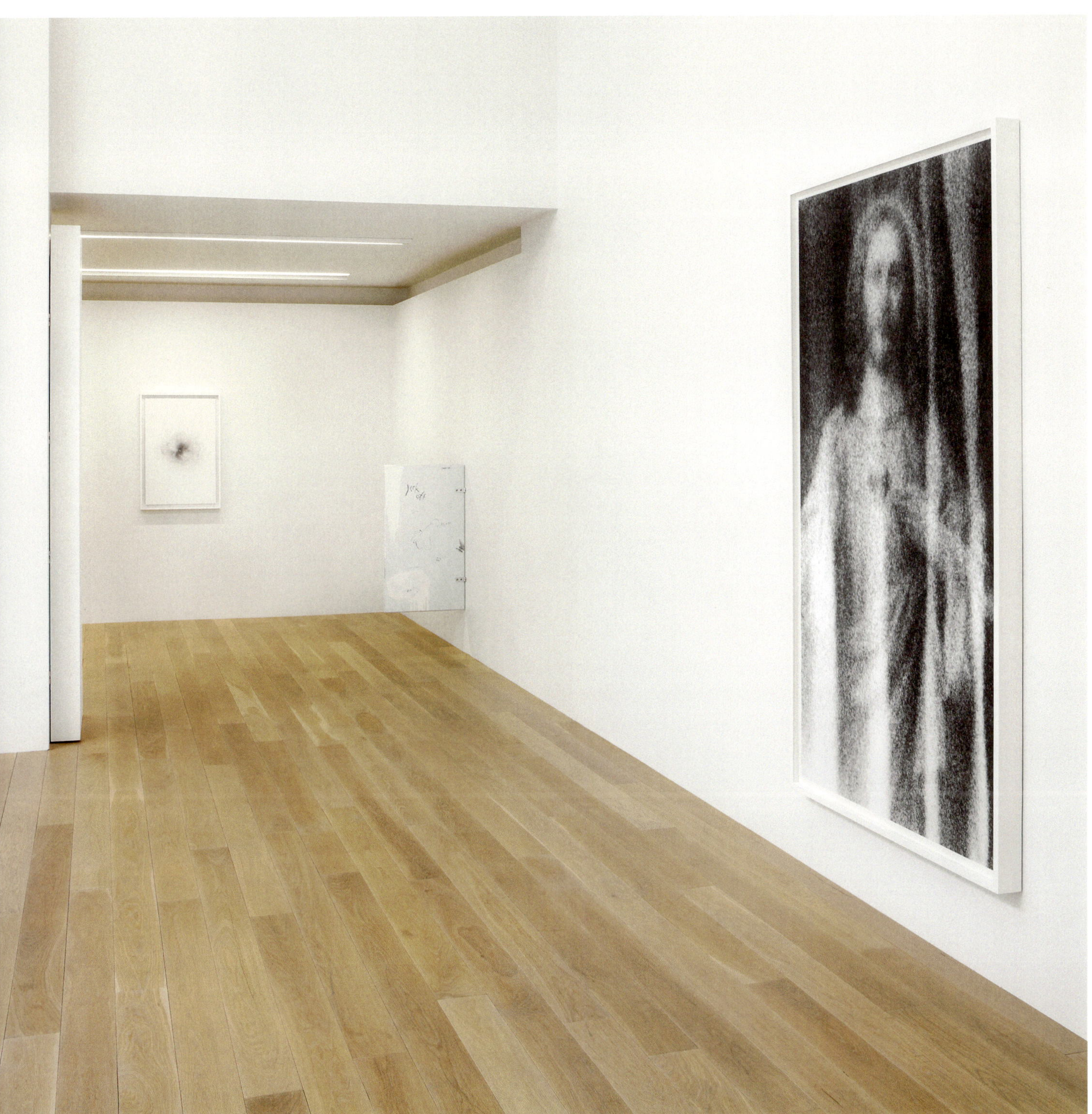

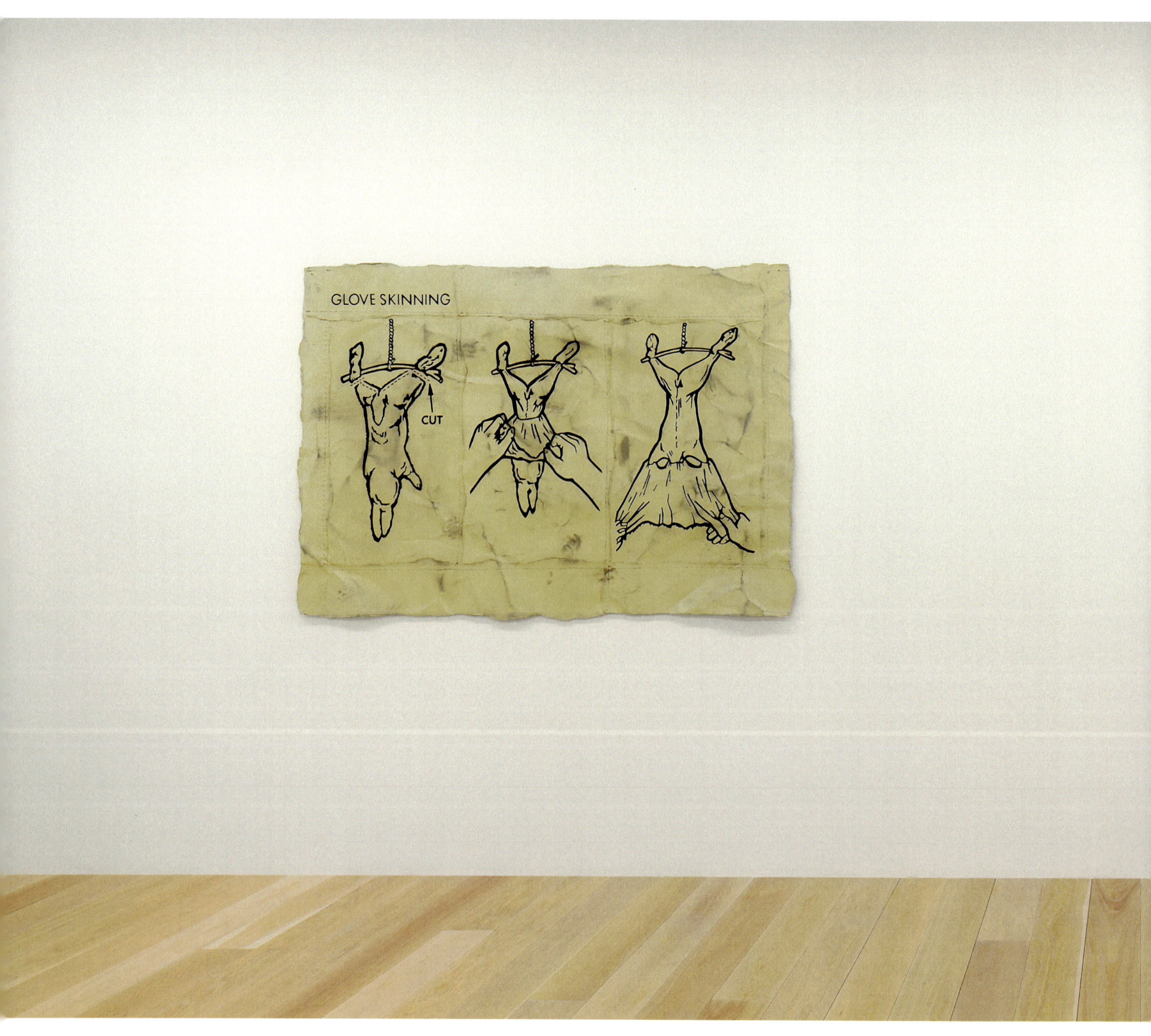
GLOVE SKINNING
CUT

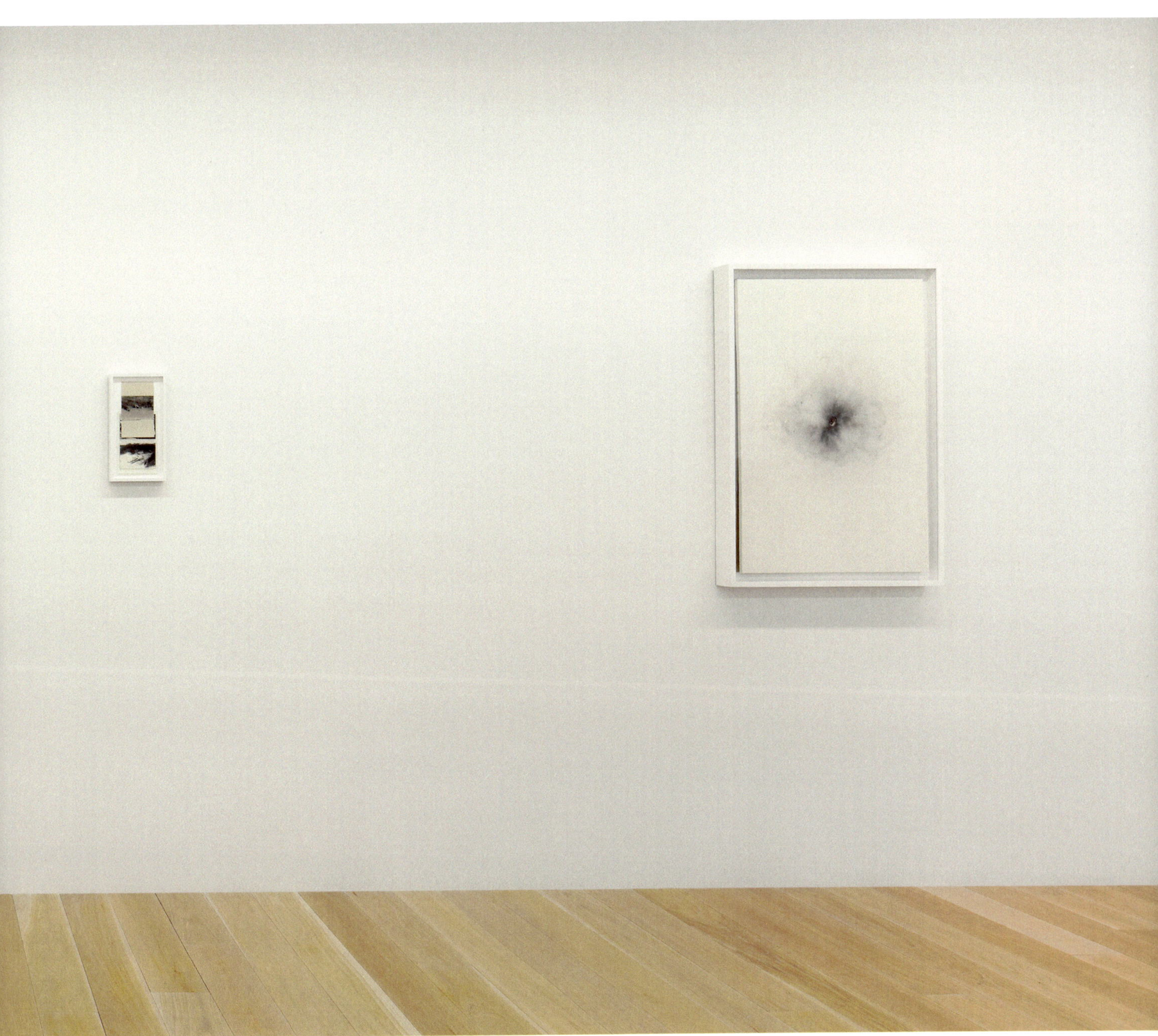

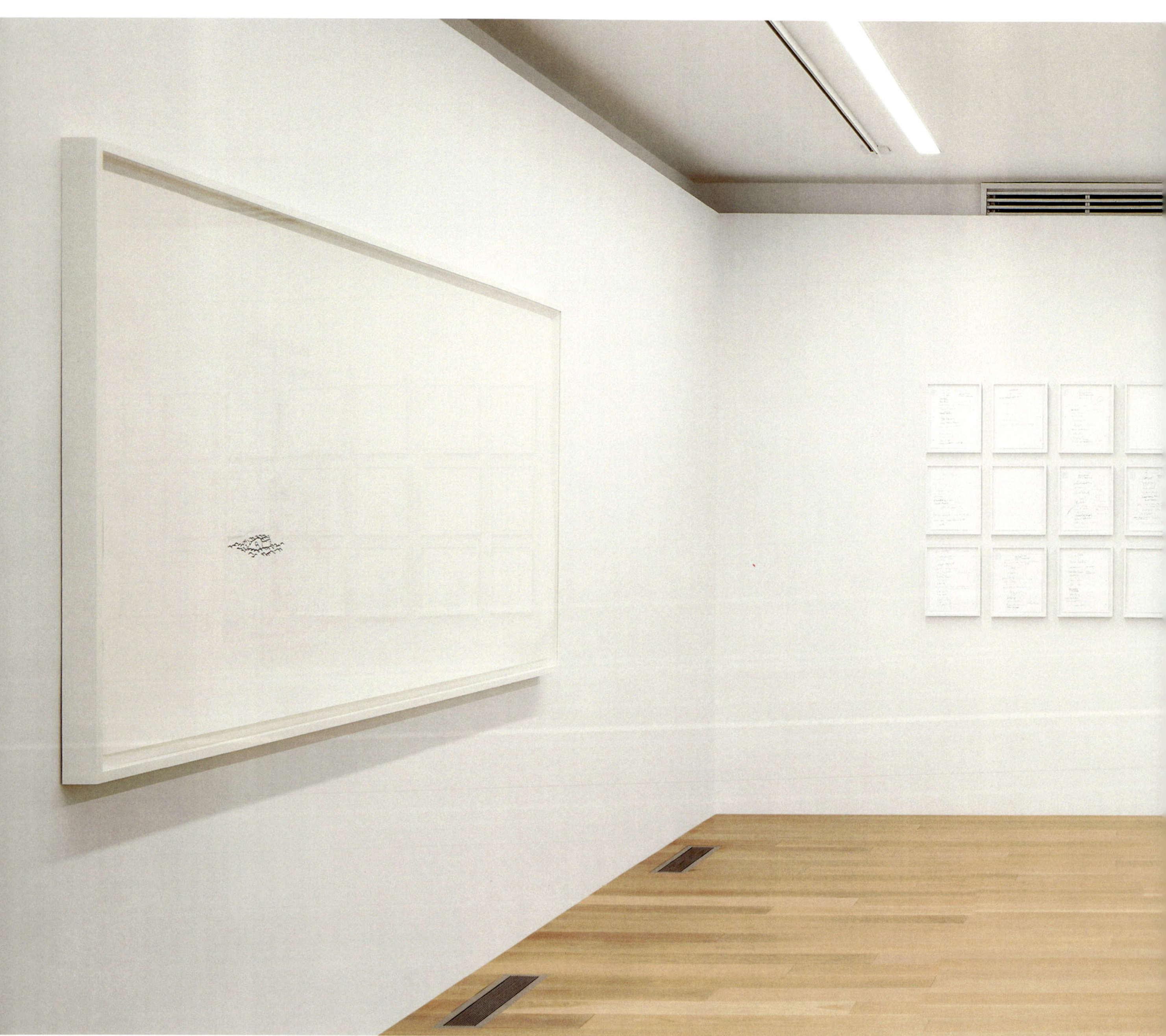

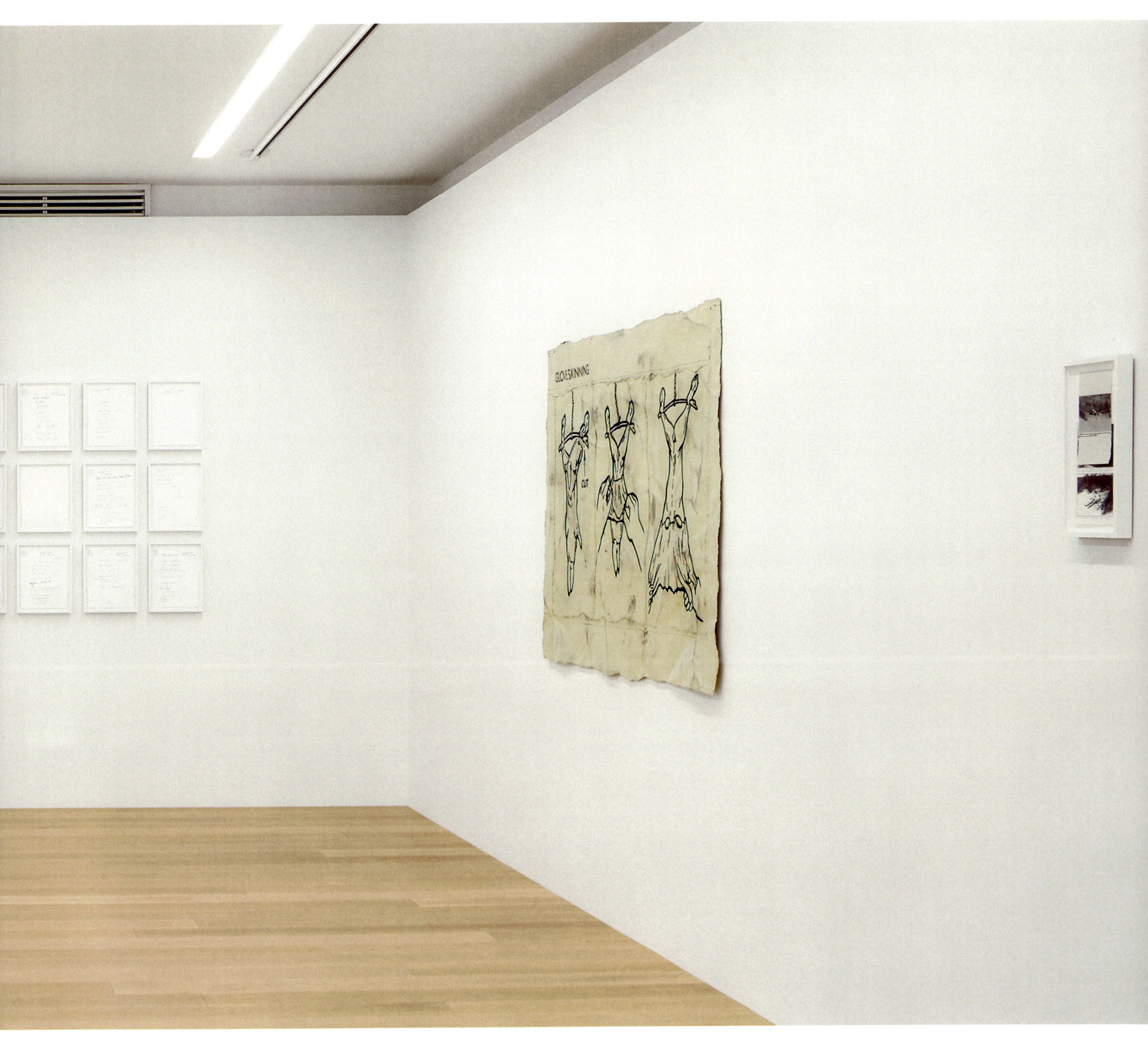
GLOVESKINNING
CUT

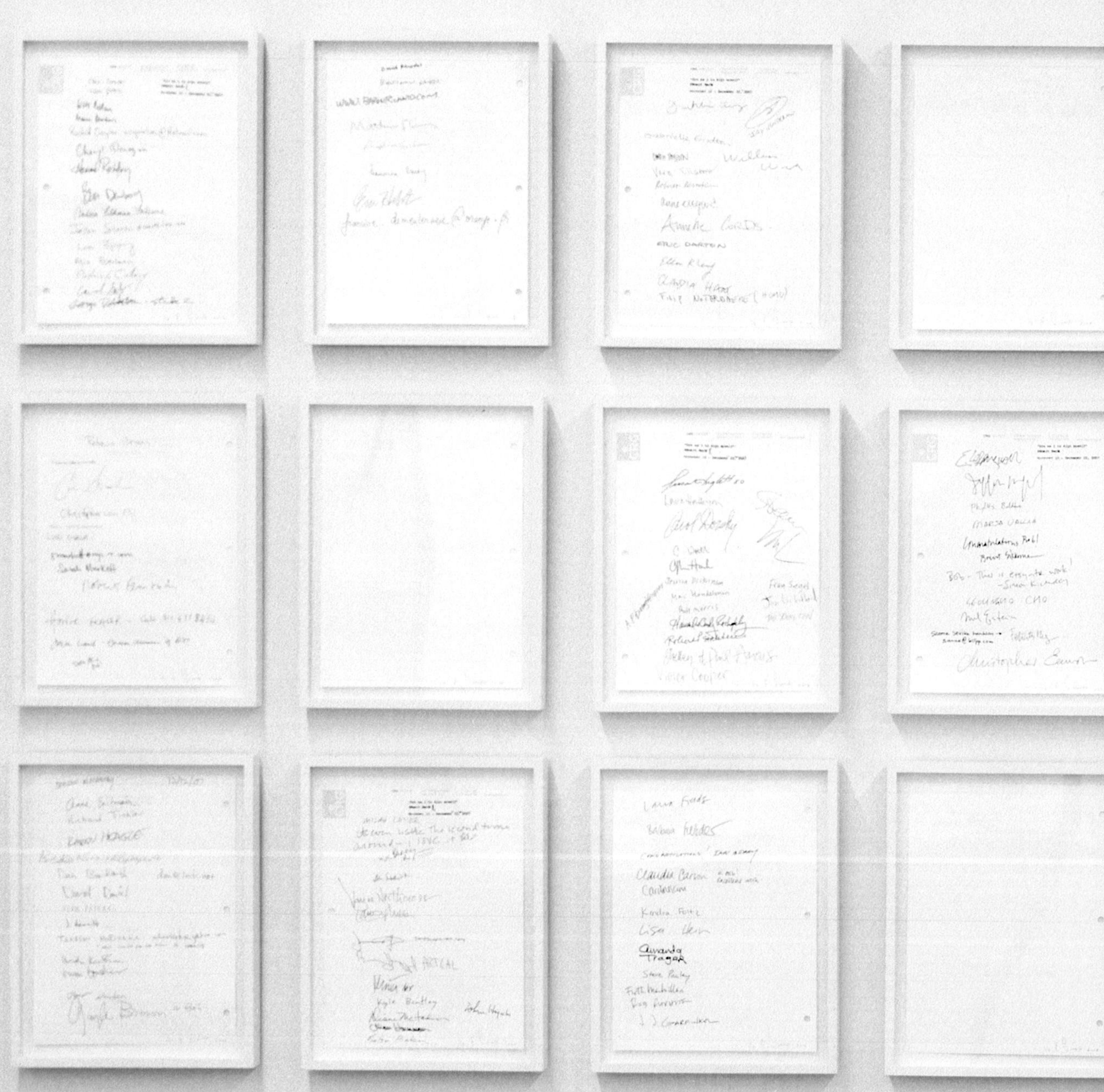

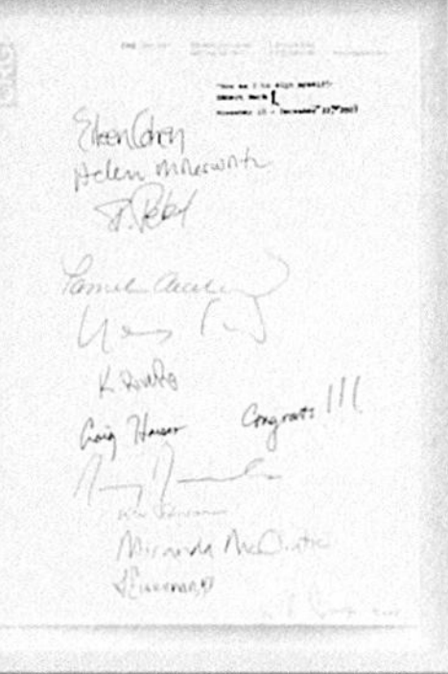
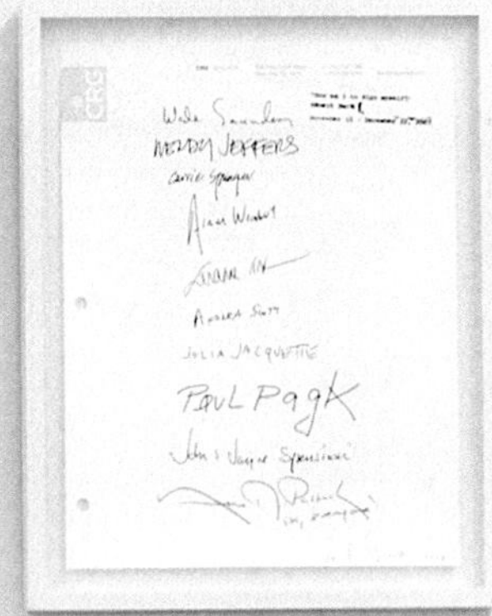
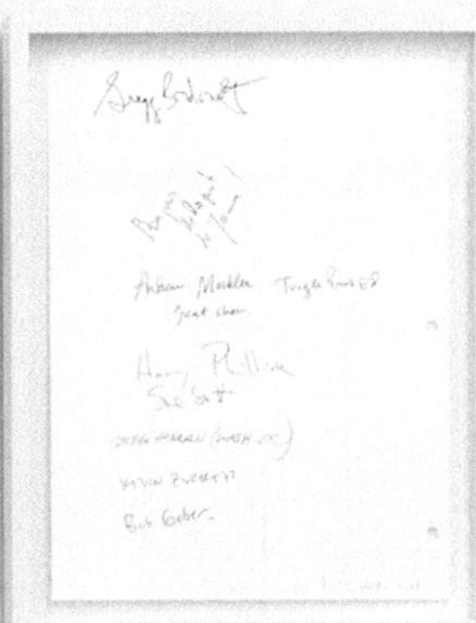

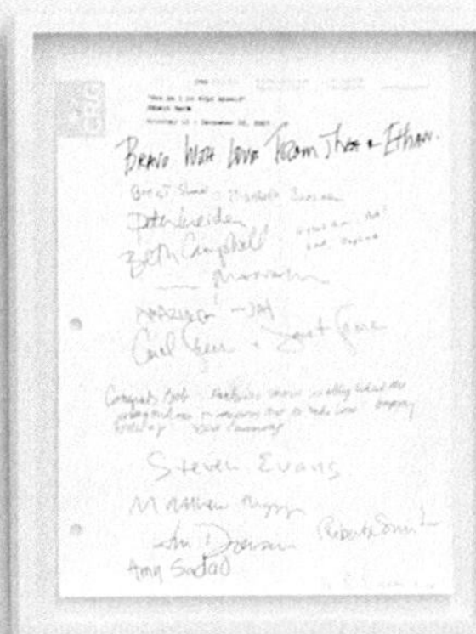
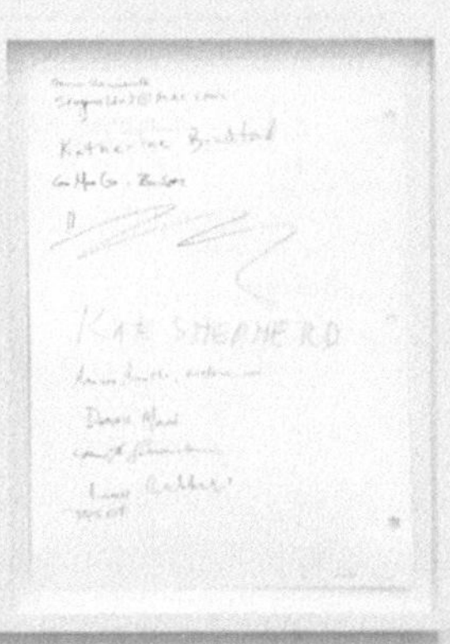
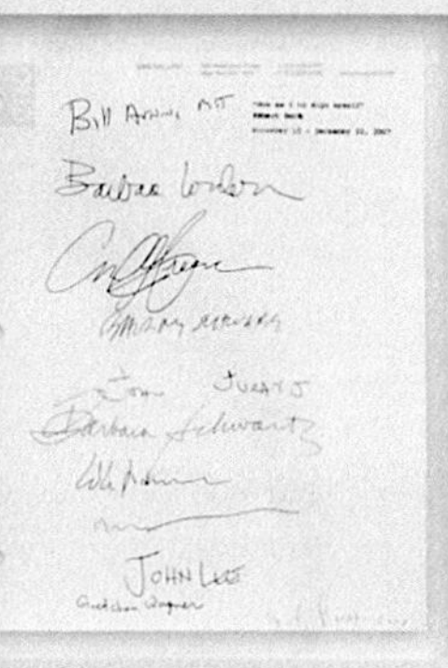
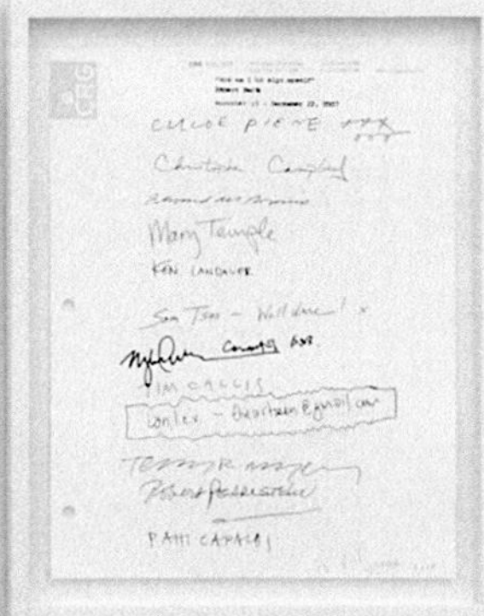
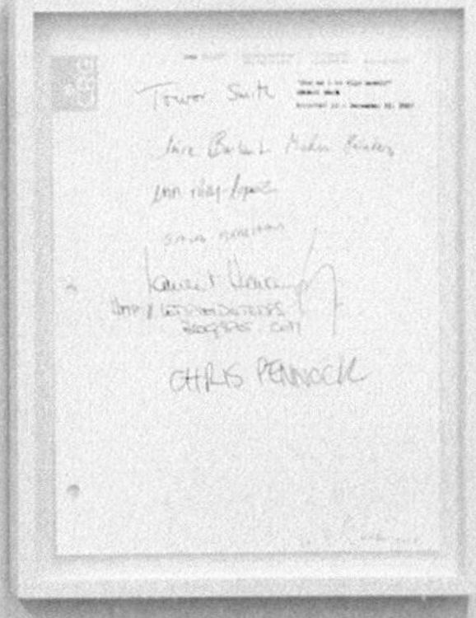
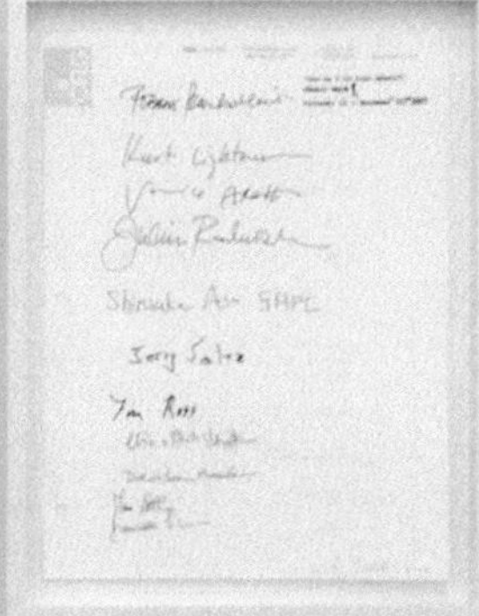

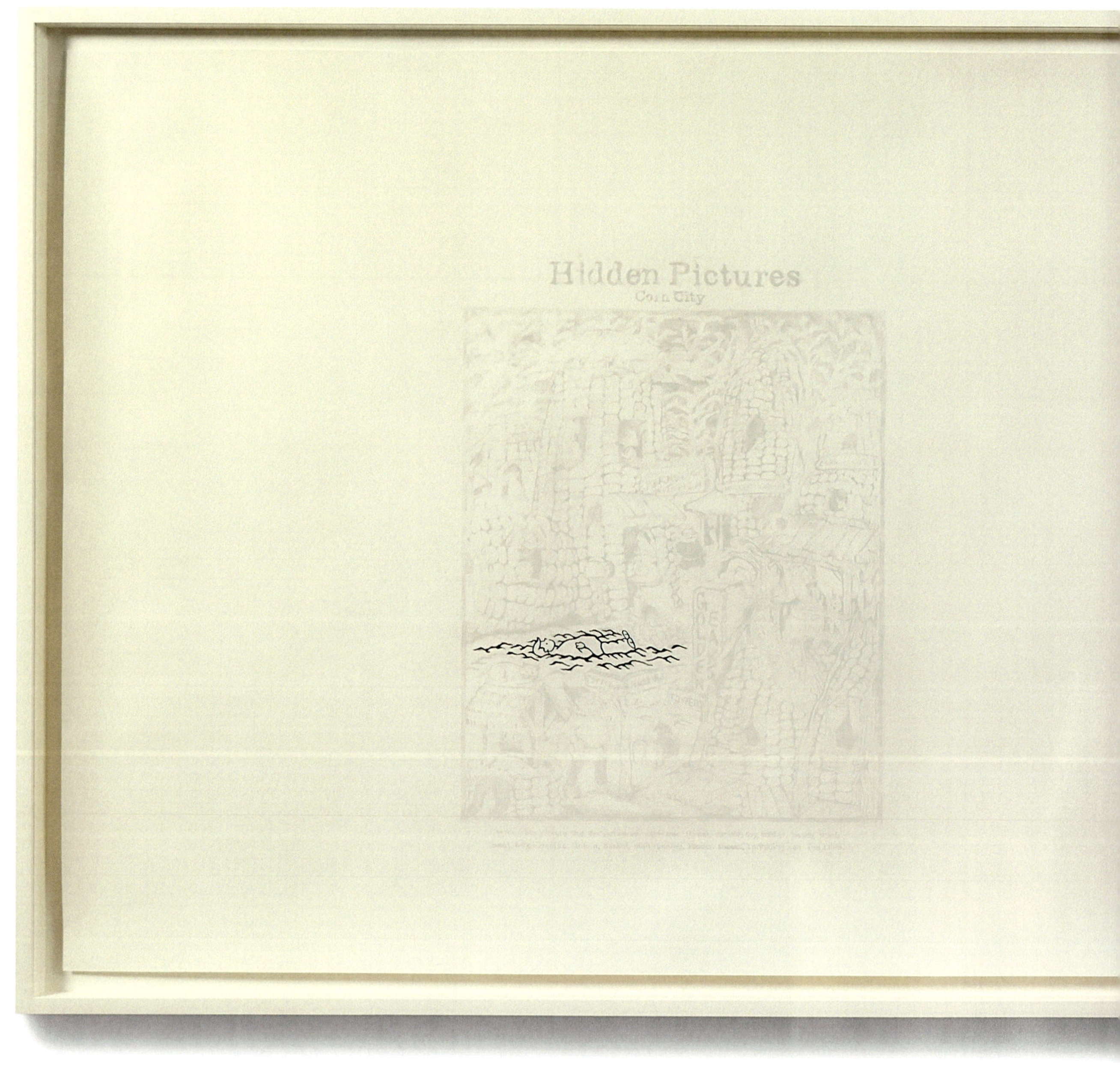
Hidden Pictures
Corn City

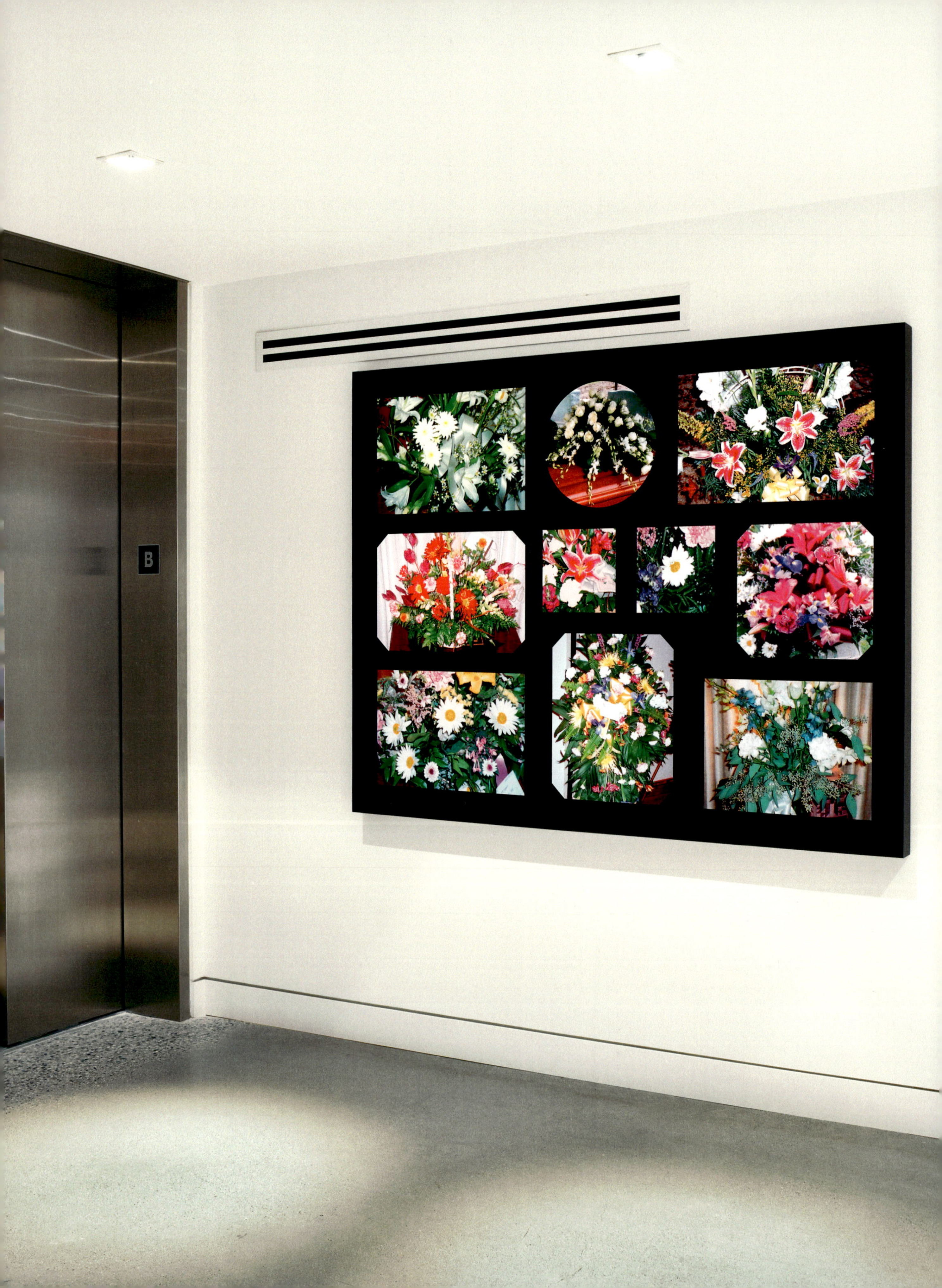

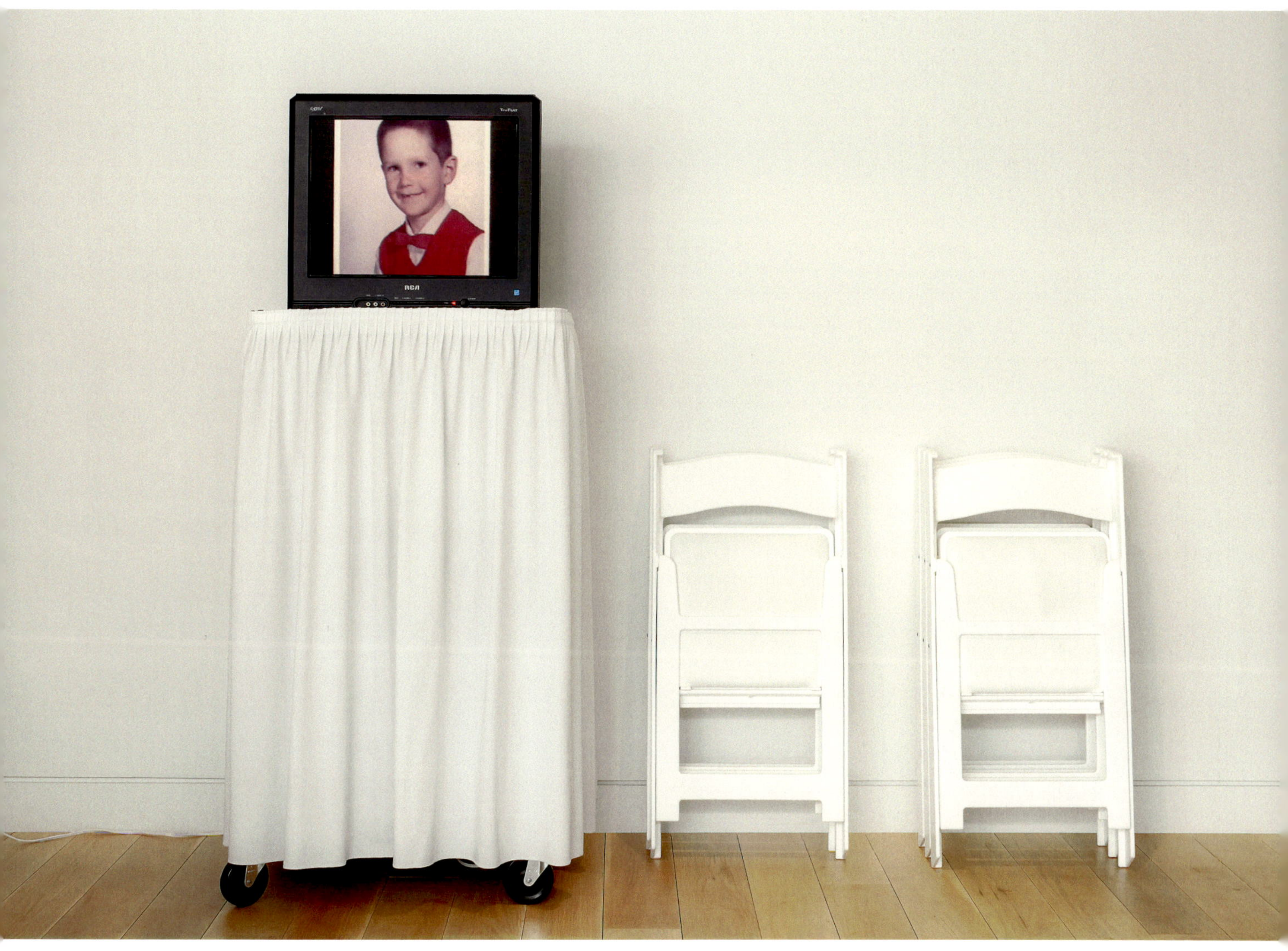

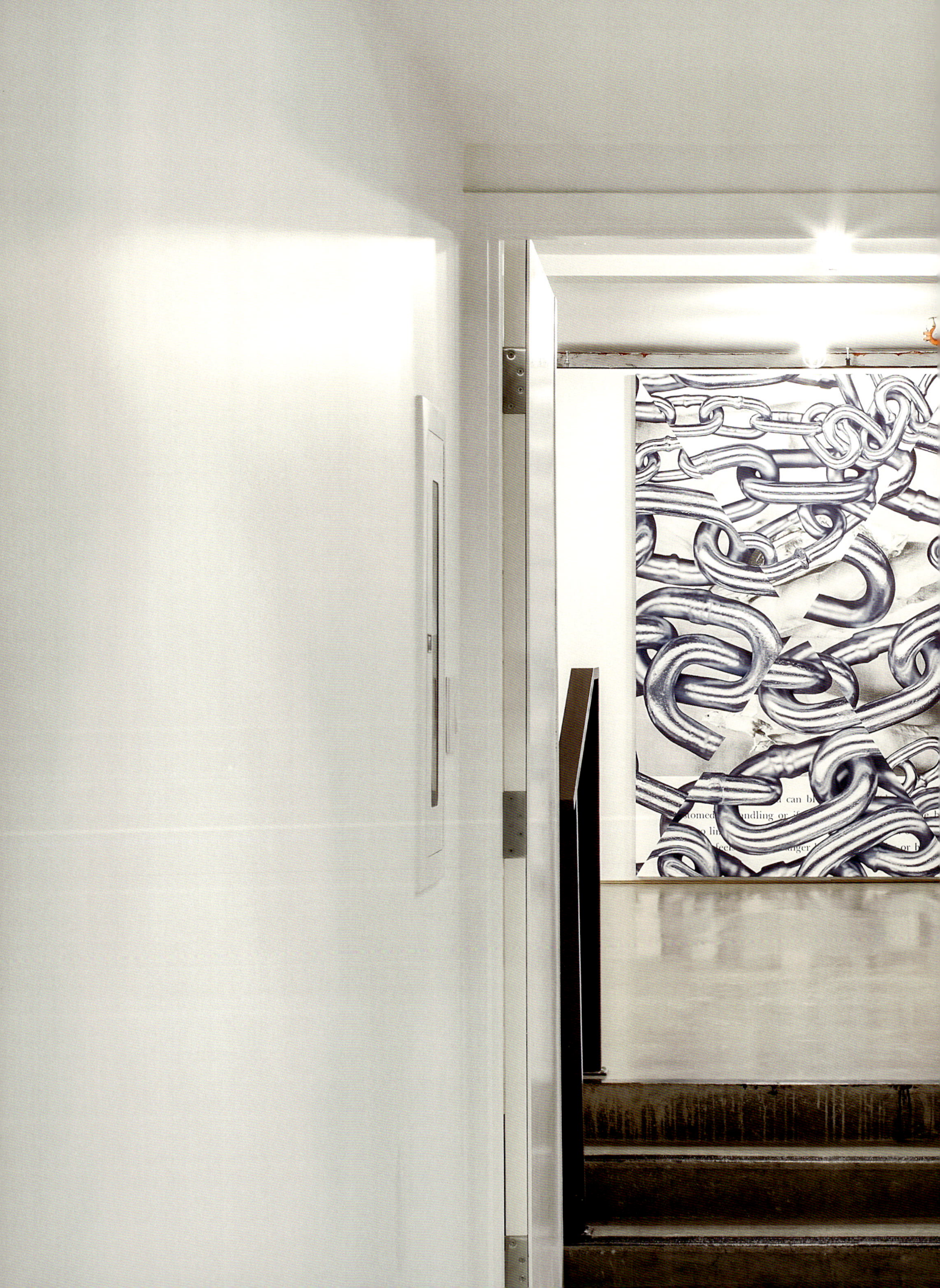

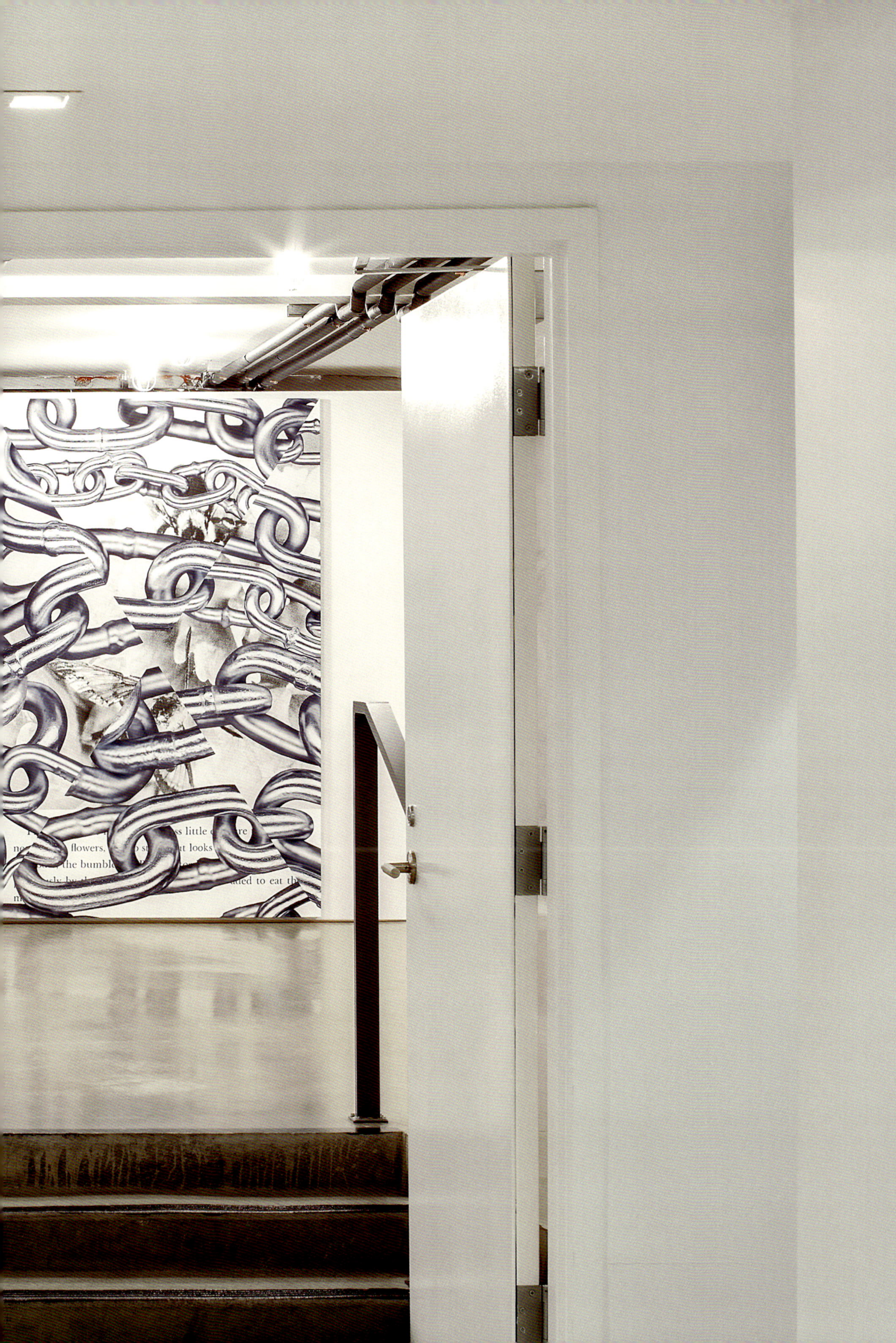
ss little c   re
ne   flowers,   o st   at looks
     the bumble
       ly by th   ded to eat th
m

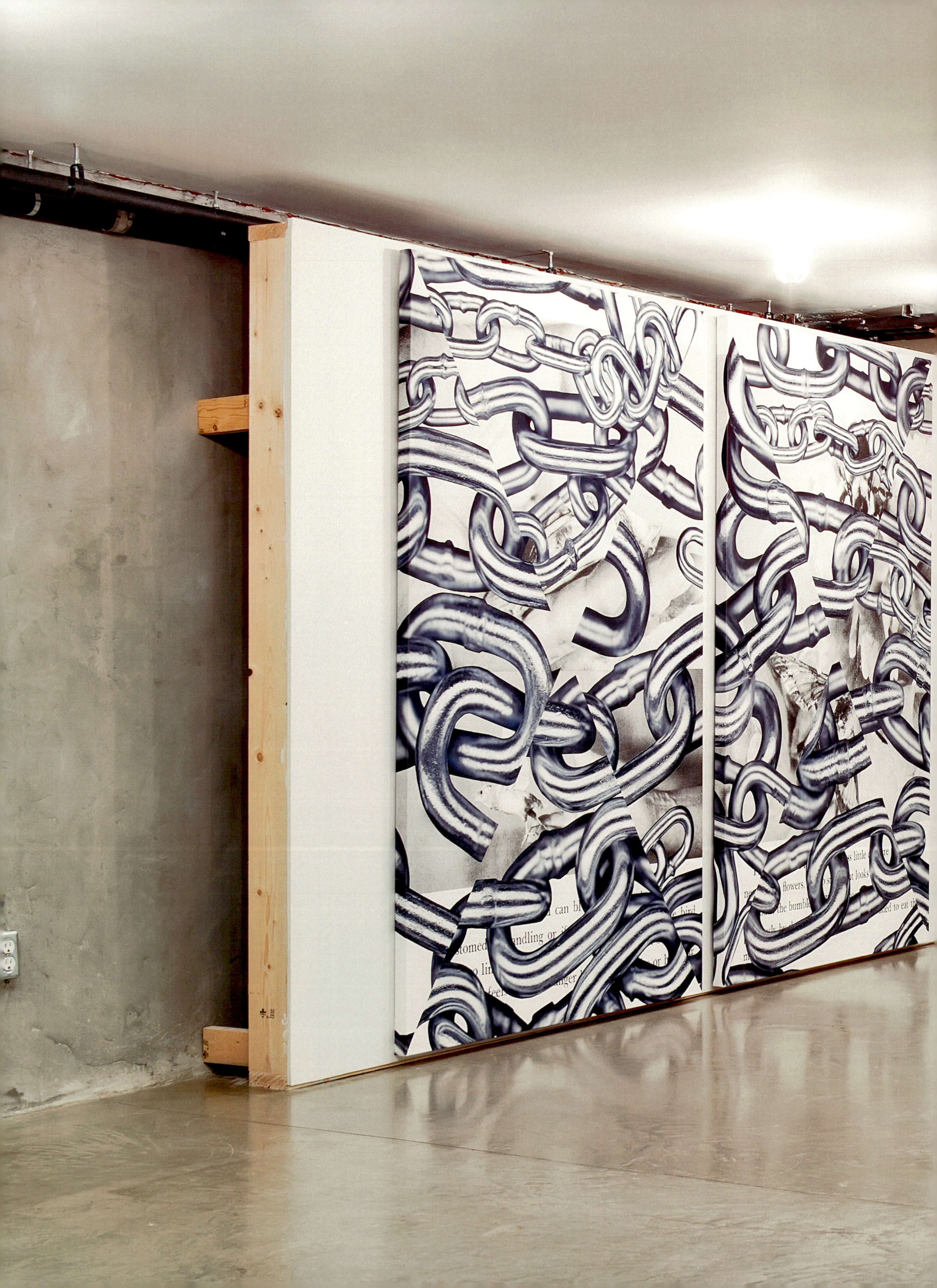

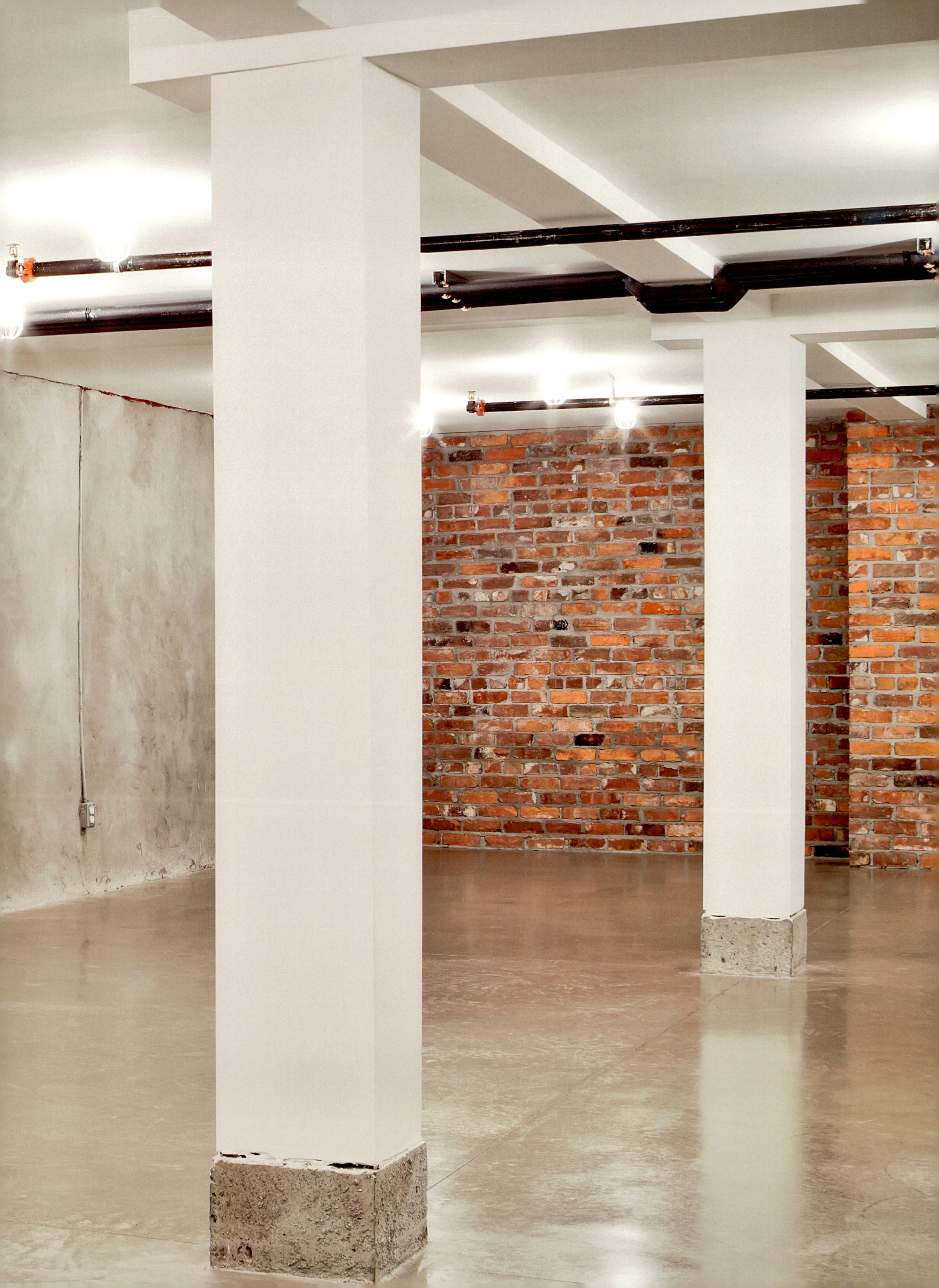

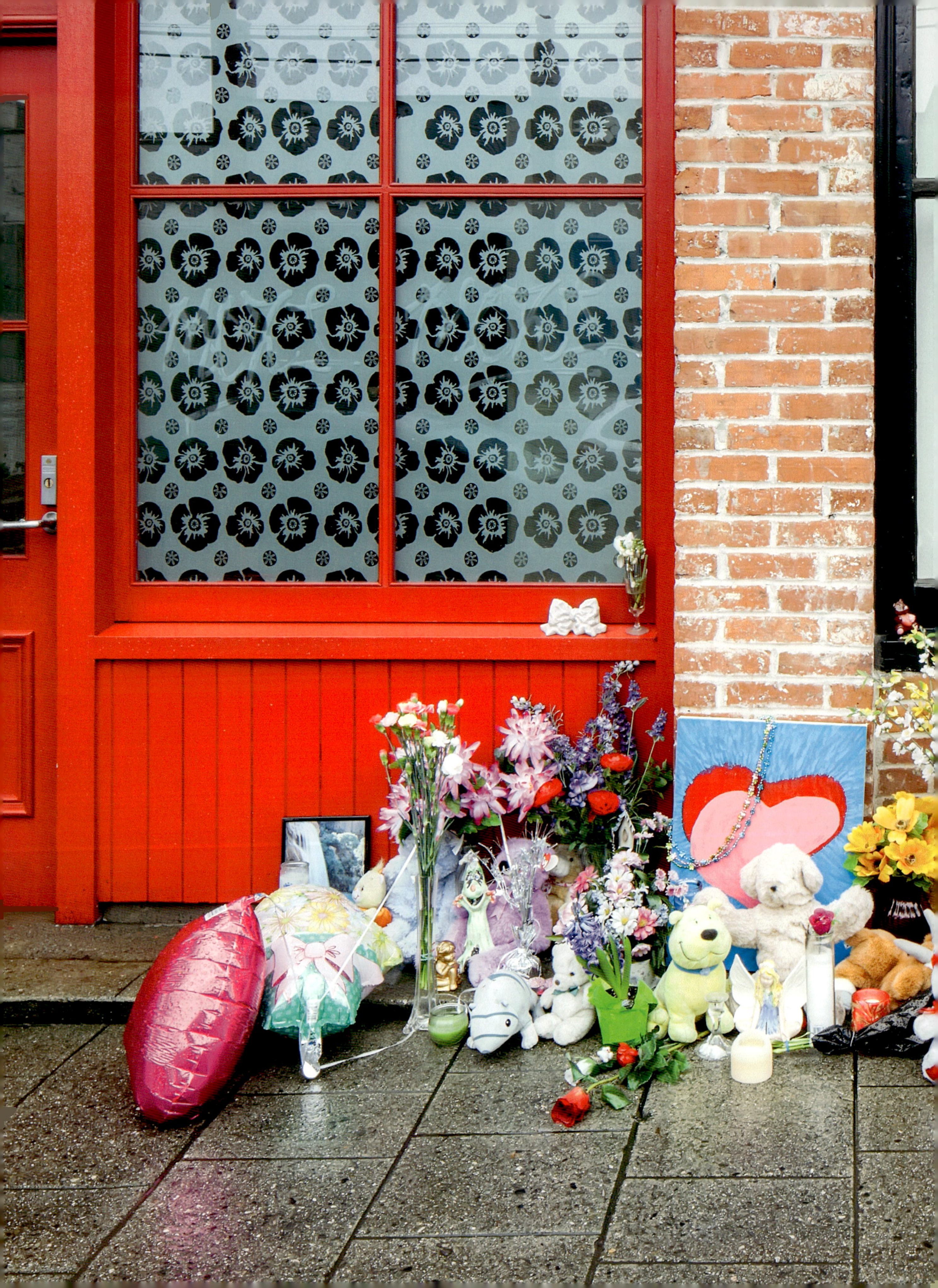

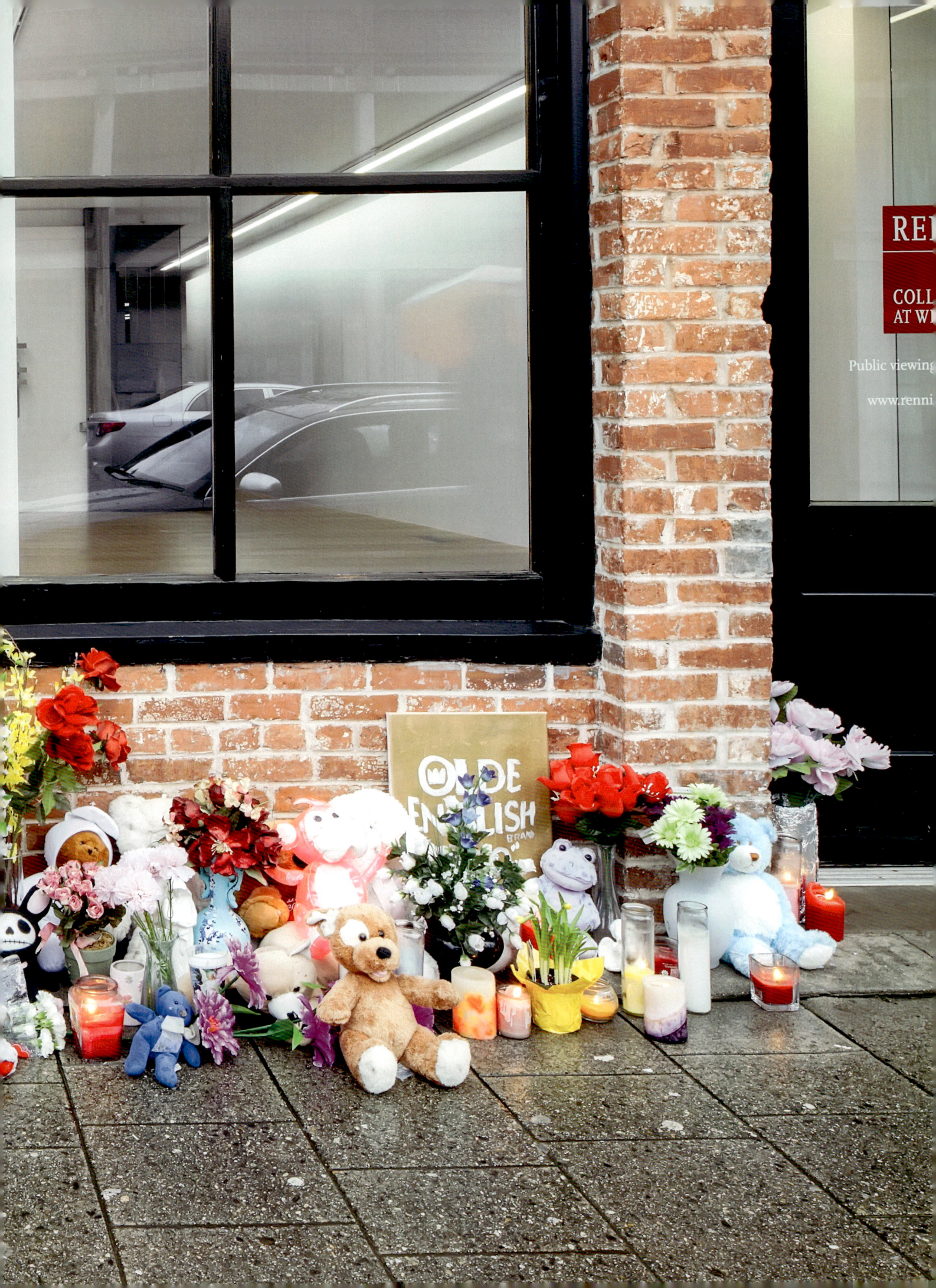
REI
COLL
AT WI
Public viewing
www.renni
OLDE
ENGLISH
BRAND

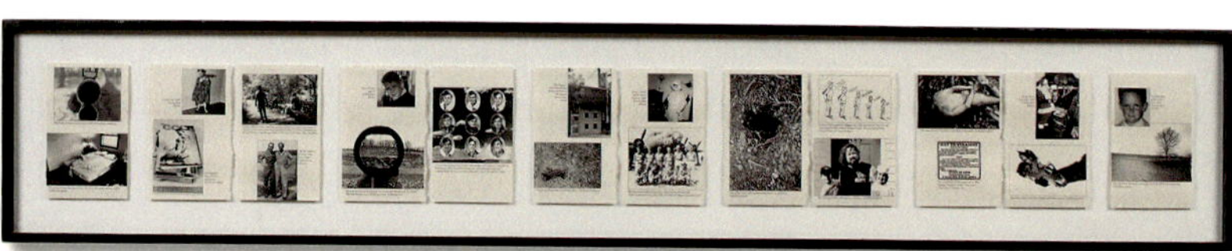

The Tail Gunner's Vulgar Revenge, 1994
twelve laser prints
11 x 64 inches
(27.9 x 162.6 cm)

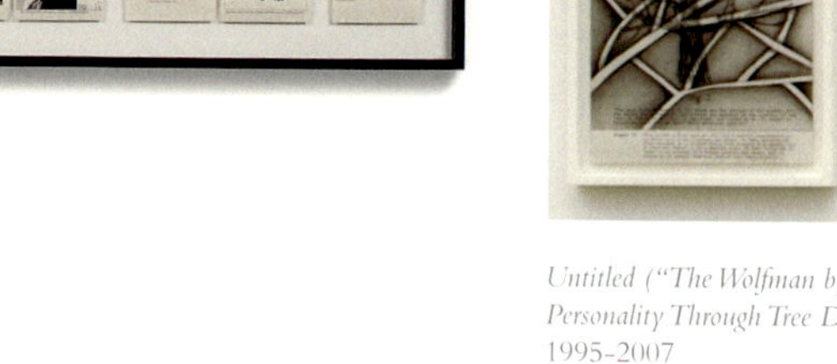

*Untitled ("The Wolfman by Sigmund Freud/"Assessing
Personality Through Tree Drawings" by Karen Bolander)*,
1995–2007
acrylic paint, charcoal, graphite, ink, and
latent fingerprint powder on paper
13 ½ x 10 ¾ inches
(34.3 x 27.3 cm)

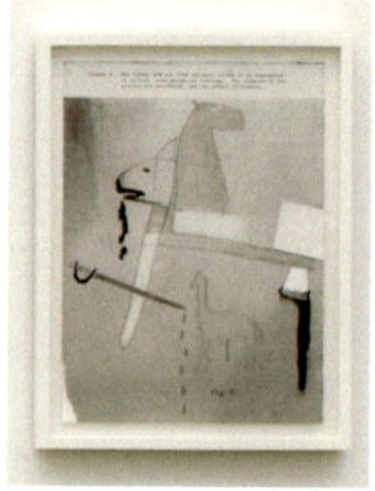

*Untitled ("Analysis of a Phobia in a Five-Year-Old Boy"
by Sigmund Freud / "Art Therapy" by Elinor Ulman and
Penny Dascinger)*, 1997/2005
latent fingerprint powder, oil pastel, acrylic paint,
graphite, carbon, tape, and charcoal on paper
13 ½ x 10 ¾ inches
(34.3 x 27.3 cm)

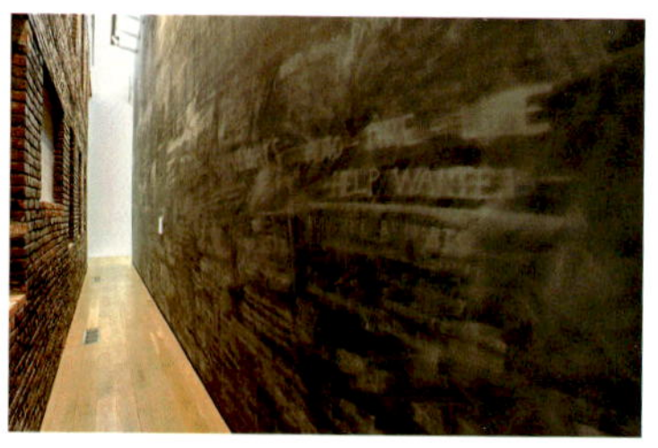

dust (Community Times, June 20, 1965), 1998/2006
mixed media
installation dimensions variable

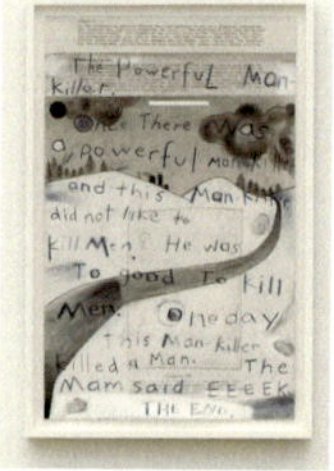

*Untitled ("The House-Tree-Person Technique: Revised
Manual" by John N. Buck"/"Assessing Personality
Through Tree Drawings" by Karen Bolander/"The
Psychoanalytic Study of the Child: Fragment of an Analysis
of an Obsessional Child" by Berta Bornstein)*, 1998–2007
acrylic paint, charcoal, conte crayon, graphite ink,
latent fingerprint powder, and tape on paper
20 ½ x 13 ¾ inches
(52.1 x 34.9 cm)

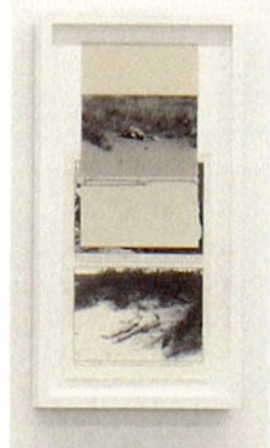

The Remnants, 1999
archival laser print and thread
13 ⅛ x 7 inches
(33.3 x 17.8 cm)

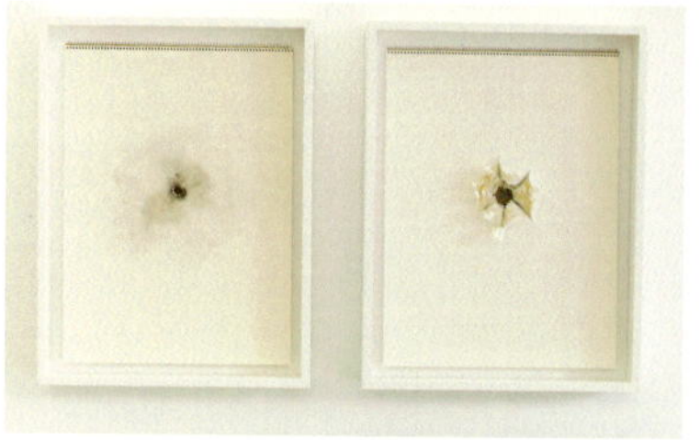

*Untitled (Daly Over/Under @ Close Range w/ .12
"Punkin" Ball Slug) (Entrance and Exit)*, 1999
gunpowder and sketchpads in two parts
27 ⅜ x 21 ¼ x 4 ⅜ inches
(69.5 x 54 x 11.1 cm)

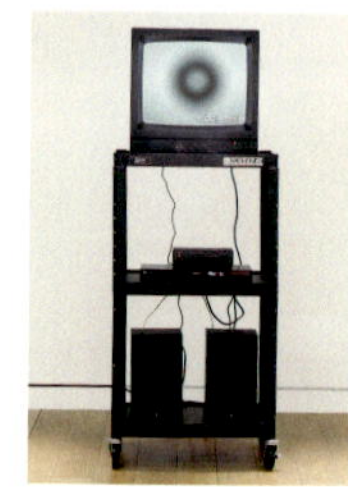

Untitled (Dec. 29, 1993), 1999
DVD, DVD player, monitor, AV cart, receiver, speakers
cart: 44 x 24 x 18 inches (111.8 x 61 x 45.7 cm)
monitor: 18 x 19 x 14 inches (45.7 x 48.3 x 35.6 cm)
Edition 2 of 3

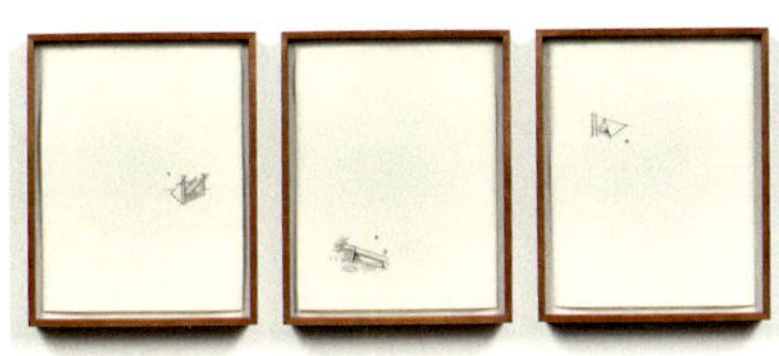

Untitled (The Modern Man's Guide to Life by Denise Boyles, Alan Rose and Alan Wellikoff), 1999
graphite on paper in three parts
15 ½ x 12 ½ inches
(39.4 x 31.8 cm)

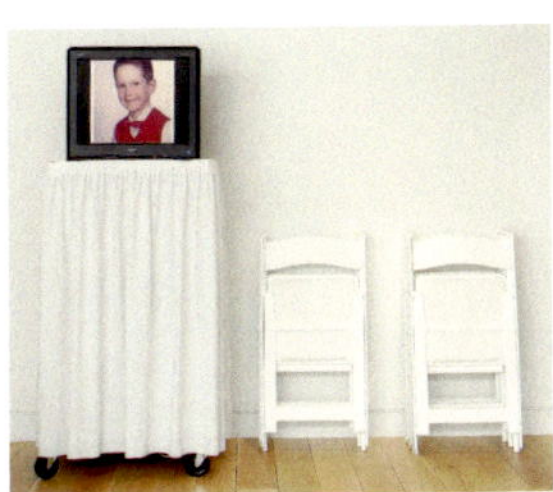

The Memorial Screening (1974), 2000
DVD, AV cart, fabric clips, chairs, DVD player,
receiver, speakers
installation dimensions variable
Edition 3 of 3

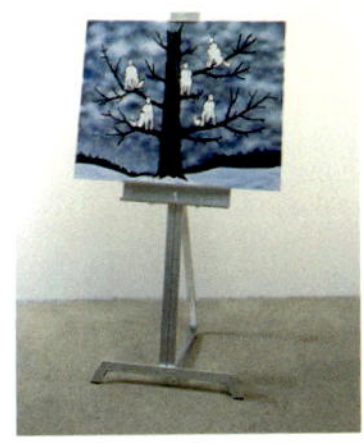

The Painting ("The Wolf Man" by the Wolf Man), 2000
oil on canvas on easel
31 x 40 inches
(78.7 x 101.6 cm)

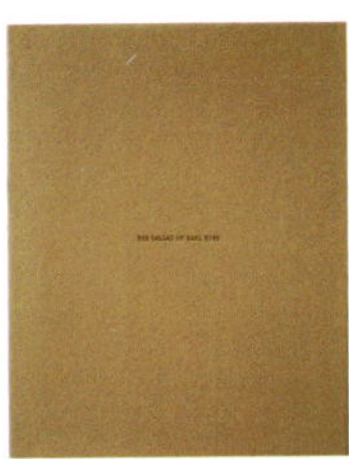

The Ballad of Earl King, 2001
cardboard box, file folder, 1 essay by Dale Peck, 2
pages ripped from books, 4 misc pages, 1 library card
file, a small gun powder paper
12 ½ x 10 x ¾ inches
(31.8 x 25.4 cm)
Edition 40 of 45

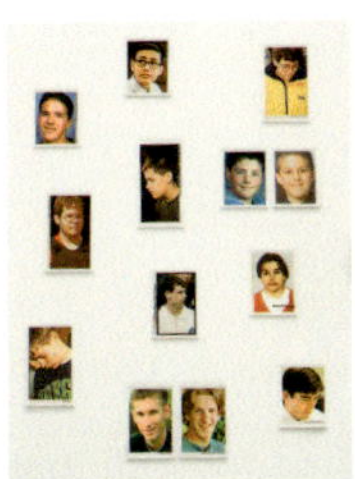

Thirteen Shooters, 2001
13 inkjet pigment prints
installation dimensions variable
David Creshaw: 81 ¼ x 45 inches (206.4 x 114.3 cm)
Reuters: 74 ⅜ x 45 inches (188.9 x 114.3 cm)
Rogelio Solis: 72 ⅜ x 45 inches (183.8 x 114.3 cm)
Sommers-Sipa: 72 x 45 inches (182.9 x 114.3 cm)
Brian Maass: 65 ⅜ x 45 inches (166.1 x 114.3 cm)
Corbis Sygma: 65 ⅜ x 45 inches (166.1 x 114.3 cm)
San Diego Union: 61 ¾ x 45 inches (156.8 x 114.3 cm)
Lafayette County: 59 ⅞ x 45 inches (152.1 x 114.3 cm)
Elaine Thompson: 57 ⅜ x 45 inches (145.7 x 114.3 cm)
Bishops Photography: 53 ⅞ x 45 inches
(136.8 x 114.3 cm)
Courtesy of the...: 53 ⅞ x 45 inches (136.8 x 114.3 cm)
Heirloom Fine: 53 ⅞ x 45 inches (136.8 x 114.3 cm)
Rose Palmisano: 53 ⅜ x 45 inches (136.2 x 114.3 cm)

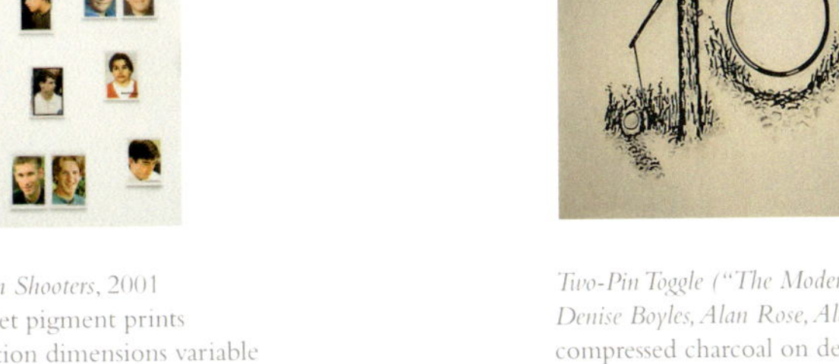

*Two-Pin Toggle ("The Modern Man's Guide to Life" by
Denise Boyles, Alan Rose, Alan Wellikoff")*, 2001
compressed charcoal on de-acidified paper
106 ½ x 121 ½ inches
(270.5 x 308.6 cm)

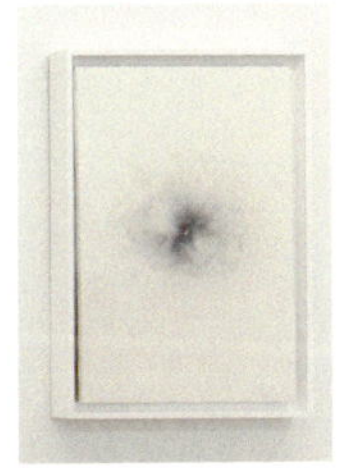

*6/20/02 - Shot No. 12 (Daly Over/Under @ Close
Range with .12 "Punkin' Ball")*, 2002
gunpowder and drawing pad
39 ¼ x 27 ¼ x 2 ⅝ inches
(99.7 x 69.2 x 6.7 cm)

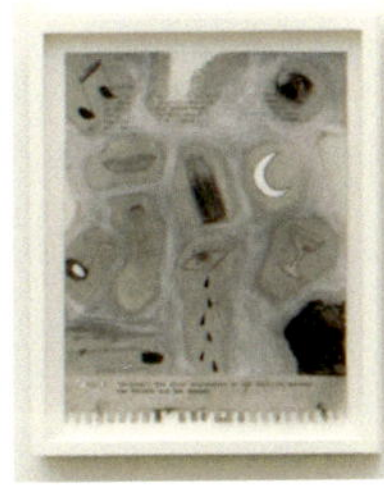

*Untitled ("Children's Drawings as Diagnostic Tests"
by Joseph H DiLeo / "Schizophrenic Art" by Margaret
Naumburg)*, 2002/2005
Conte Crayon, fingerprint ink, latent fingerprint
powder, oil pastel, acrylic paint, graphite, carbon and
charcoal on paper
11 ¼ x 9 ¾ inches
(29.8 x 24.8 cm)

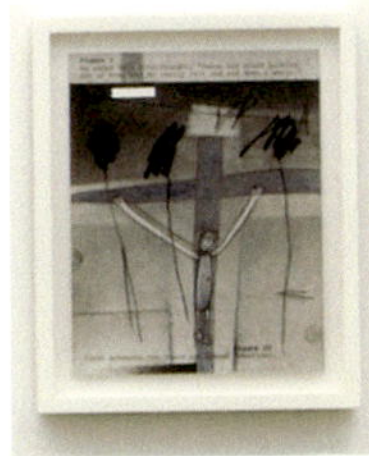

*Untitled ("Children's Art" by Miriam Lindstrom/"Their
Eyes Meeting the World: The Drawings and Paintings of
Children" by Robert Coles)*, 2002-2007
acrylic paint, charcoal, colored pencil, conte crayon,
graphite, ink, latent fingerprint powder, and tape on paper
9 ¼ x 7 ¾ inches
(23.5 x 19.7 cm)

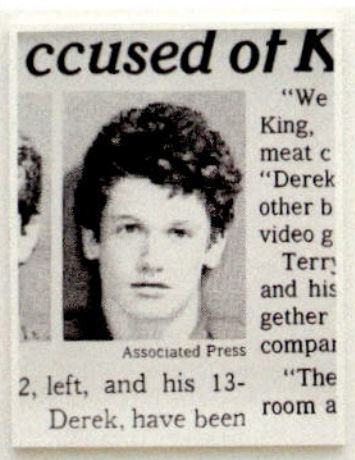

'ccused of K (The New York Times, Nov 30, 2002), 2003
oil pastel crayon on paper
103 x 83 ½ x 3 ½ inches
(261.6 x 212.1 x 8.9 cm)

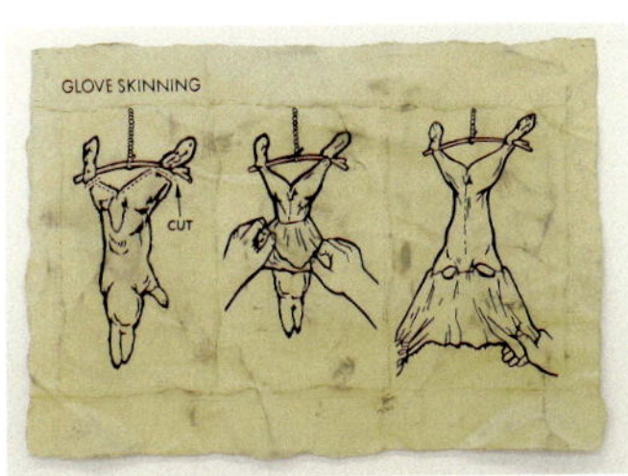

*"Glove Skinning" (Bruised) ("The Modern Man's Guide
to Life' by Denise Boyles, Alan Rose, and Alan Wellikoff)*,
2003
charcoal and thread on paper
43 ½ x 64 inches
(110.5 x 162.6 cm)

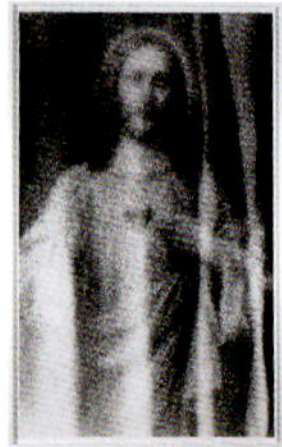

Screen Memory (Mother's Room), 2003
silver gelatin print
88 ½ x 56 inches
(224.8 x 142.2 cm)
Edition 2 of 5

Wall Hung Urinal Screen ("Big Red"), 2003
steel, particle board, laminated plastic, ink,
and graphite
41 ½ x 24 x 1 inches
(105.4 x 61 x 2.5 cm)

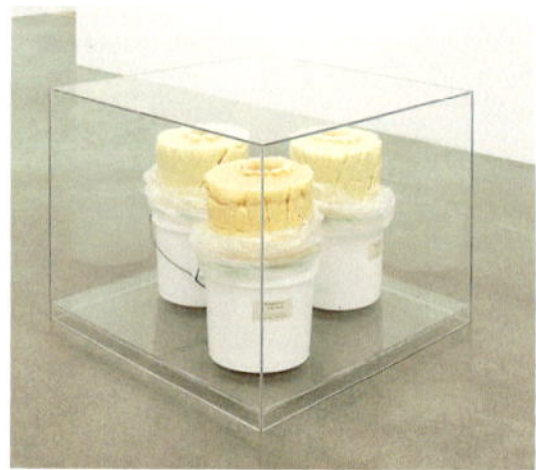

*01/25/04 - Shots No. 12, 13, 14 (Daly Over/Under at
Close Range with .12 Gauge "Punkin' Ball" Slug)*, 2004
wound filler, plastic, metal, and paper in three parts
20 x 14 x 14 inches
(50.8 x 35.6 x 35.6 cm)

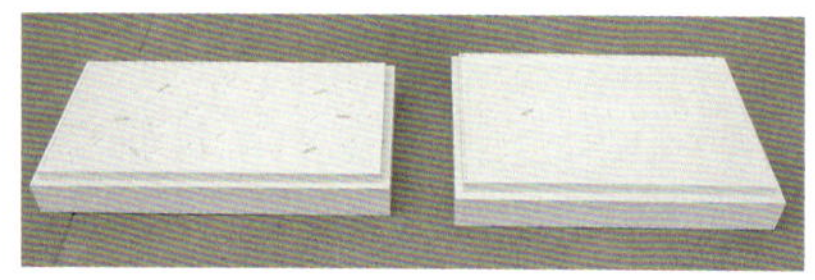

Artwork by Kip Kinkel For His Parents, Bill and Faith,
2004
wood plinths, silicone, and wound filler
19 ¾ x 67 ½ x 3 ½ inches
(50.2 x 171.4 x 8.9 cm)
Edition 1 of 3

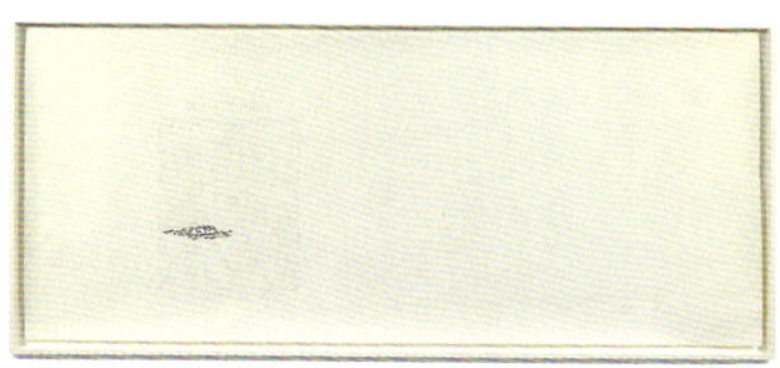

"Hidden Pictures" (At Rest), 2004
graphite on paper
47 ½ x 111 x 2 ½ inches
(120.7 x 281.9 x 6.3 cm)

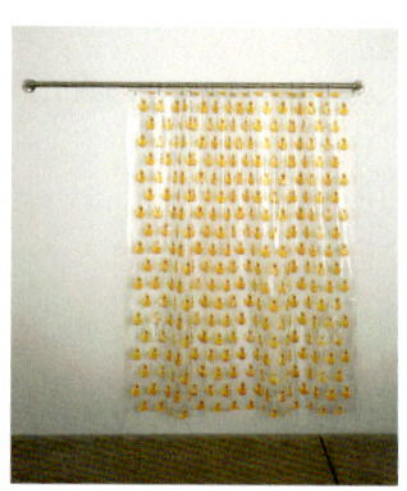

"Private Zone" (White), 2004
screen print on vinyl shower curtain and metal rod
75 ½ x 80 ½ x 3 ½ inches
(191.8 x 204.5 x 8.9 cm)
Edition 2 of 3

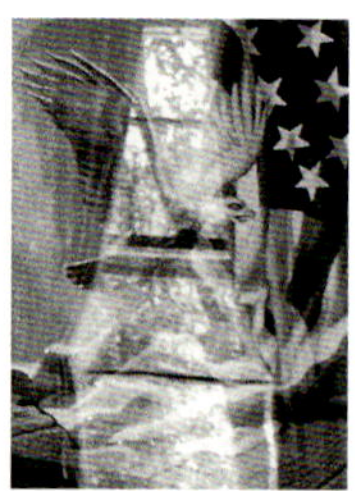

Screen Memory (Brother's Room), 2004
silver gelatin print
74 x 55 ¾ inches
(188 x 141.6 cm)
Edition 2 of 5

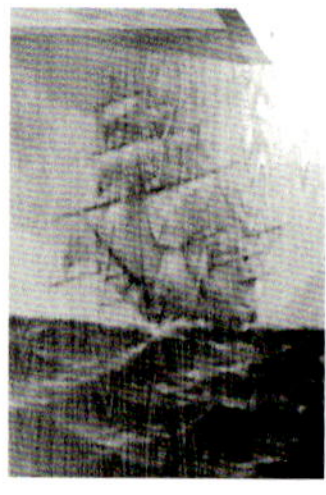

Screen Memory (Family Room), 2004
silver gelatin print
79 ½ x 56 inches
(201.9 x 142.2 x 8.3 cm)
Edition 2 of 5

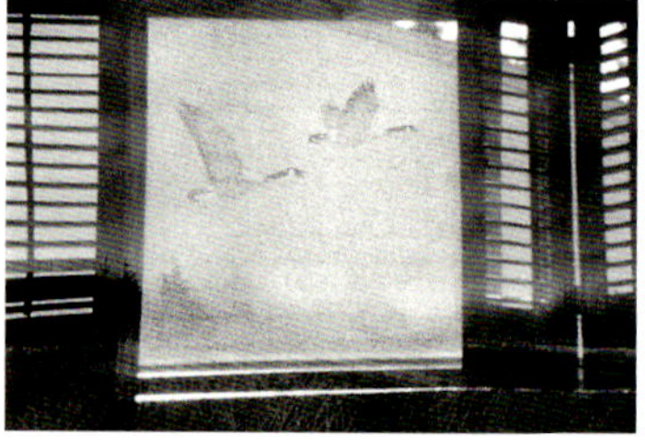

Screen Memory (Father's Room), 2004
silver gelatin print
55 3/4 x 80 1/4 inches
(141.6 x 203.8 cm)
Edition 2 of 5

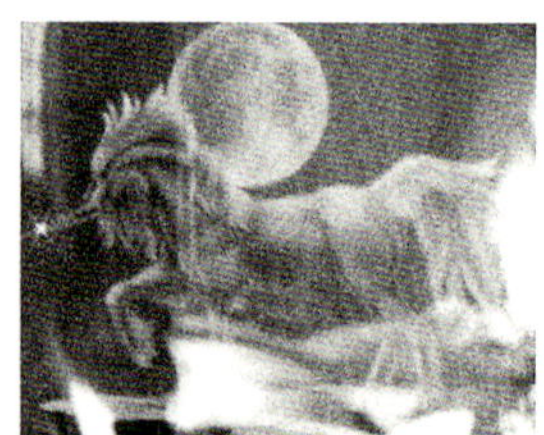

Screen Memory (Sister's Room), 2004
silver gelatin print
55 ¾ x 69 inches
(141.6 x 175.3 cm)
Edition 2 of 5

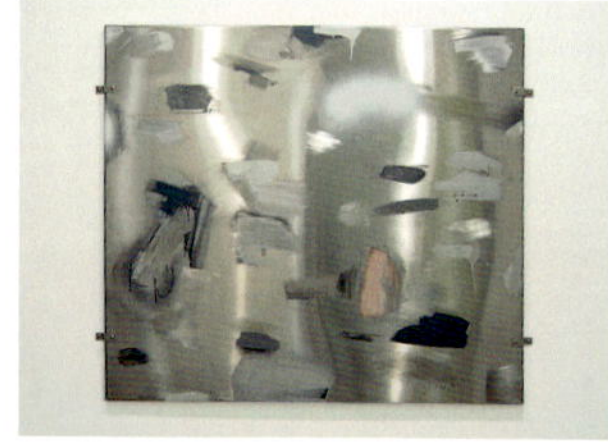

Untitled (Clean), 2004
mixed media on stainless steel
57 ¾ x 65 ¾ x ¾ inches
(146.7 x 167 x 1.9 cm)

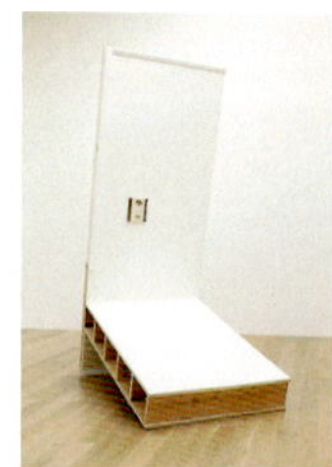

Wall Ceiling ("Bless This House..."), 2004
mixed media
126 x 48 x 80 inches
(320 x 121.9 x 203.2 cm)

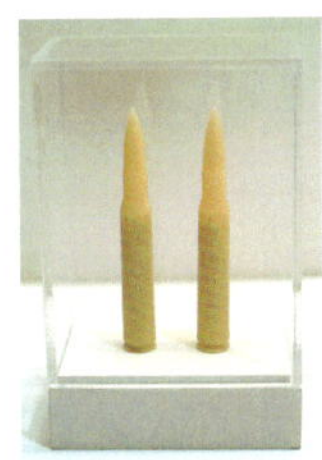

Wound Fillers ("Loves Me"/"Loves Me Not"), 2004
wound filler, wood, Plexiglass and metal
5 x 3 ¼ x 2 ⅛ inches
(12.7 x 8.3 x 5.4 cm)
Edition 3 of 5

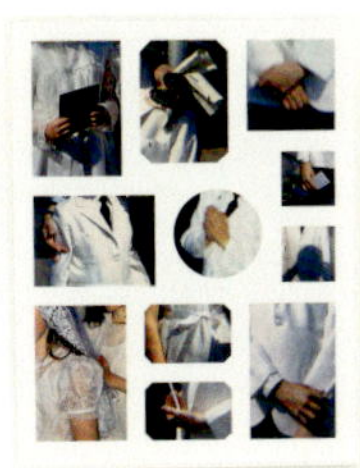

A Part From the Whole (Communion), 2005
11 chromogenic prints, wood, matte board
76 x 60 ½ x 2 ¾ inches
(193 x 153.7 x 7 cm)
Edition 3 of 6

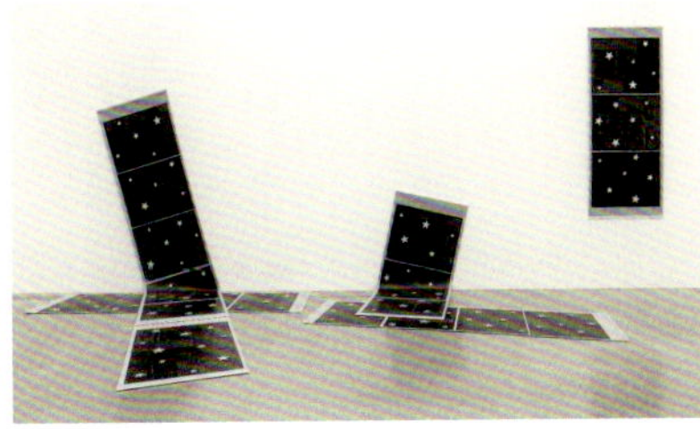

Bars and Stars ("The Daily Mirror", May 1, 2004), 2006
silkscreen on six off-set printing blankets and anodised
aluminum stars
Each: 37 ¾ inches (95.9 cm) wide x varying lengths

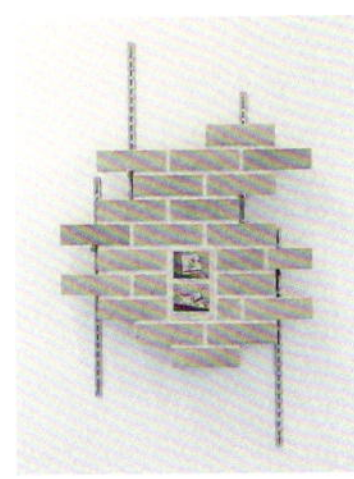

*Brick and Bracket ("Kill Grandma For Me"
by Jim DeFilice)*, 2006
steel, hydrocal, polymer ink
44 x 27 ¼ x 5 ½ inches
(111.8 x 69.2 x 14 cm)
Edition 1 of 3

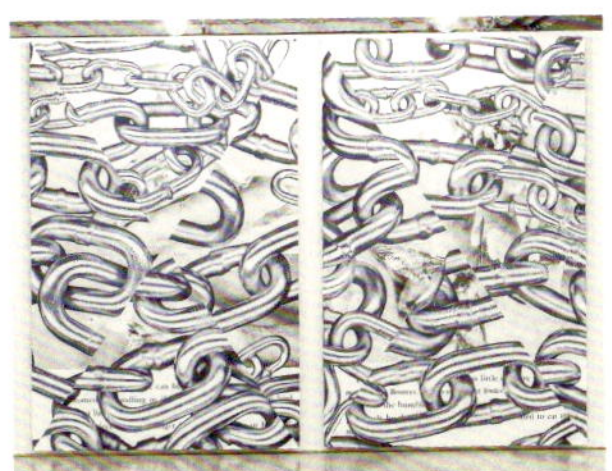

*Feign of Association ("Animals That Hide, Imitate
and Bluff" by Lilo Hess)*, 2008
crystal pigment print and synthetic polymer ink
on canvas
each panel: 81 x 54 ½ inches
(205.7 x 138.4 cm)
Edition 1 of 4

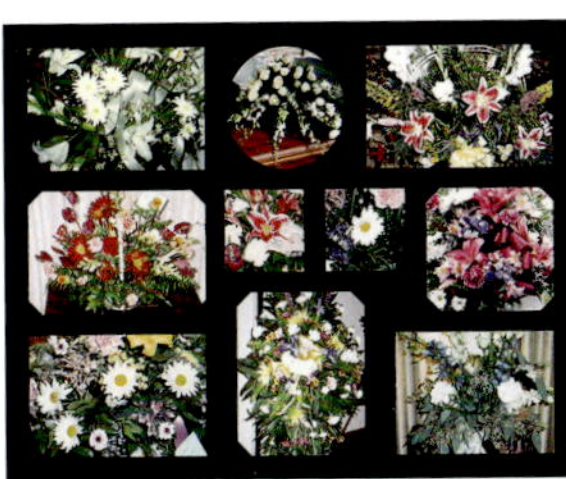

The Flowers of Upheaval (Apart from the Whole), 2006
10 chromogenic prints, satin, mat board, wood,
plexiglass
53 ¼ x 68 ⅝ inches
(135.3 x 174.3 cm)
Edition 5 of 6

Robert Buck
How Am I to Sign Myself, 2008
lithography, digital and stamp printing on
CRG letterhead in 24 parts
each: 11 x 8 ½ inches (27.9 x 21.6 cm)
Edition 1 of 2

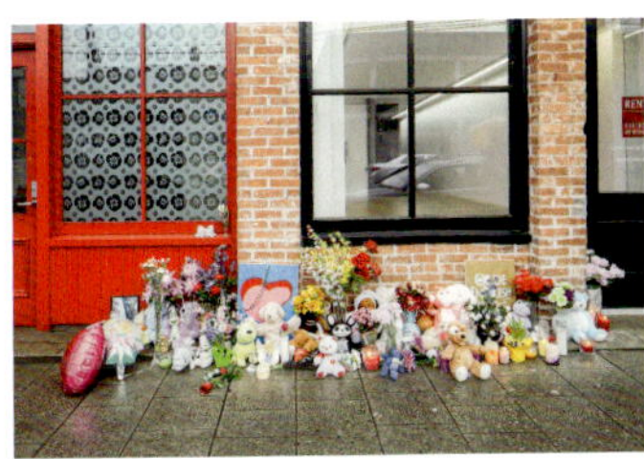

Robert Buck
The Shrine (from e to u), 2000/2012
flowers, candles, stuffed animals, balloons, thrift
store artifacts, etc.
dimensions variable
Edition 1 of 3

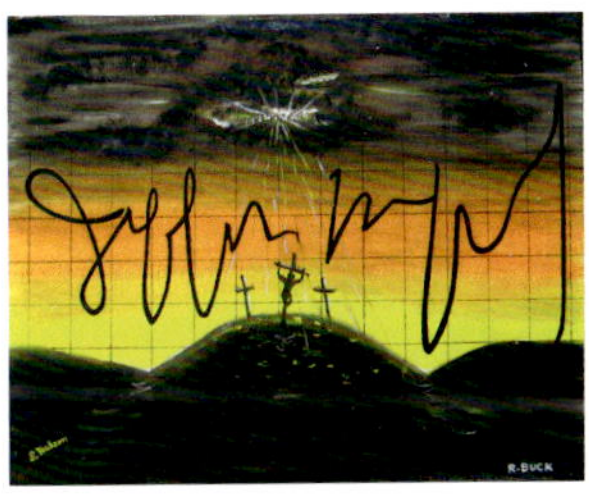

Robert Buck
Second Hand (Jeffrey Hoffeld), 2010
oil paint and india ink on found painting
(oil on canvas board)
11 ¾ x 14 ¾ inches
(29.8 x 37.5 cm)

BIOGRAPHY

Robert Buck

2008 Robert Buck replaces Robert Beck
Lives and works in New York City and Far West Texas

Solo Exhibitions

2012
Kahpenakwп [West], CRG Gallery, New York

2009
iPainting, Anthony Meier Fine Arts, San Francisco

2008
第二自然, [Second Nature], CRG Gallery, New York

Selected Group Exhibitions

2013
Inaugural Exhibition: Looking Forward, Pizzuti Collection, Columbus, OH
Alchemical, Steven Kasher Gallery, New York, curated by Kevin Moore
Booth 548, CRG Gallery, New York

2012
No Person May Carry a Fish into a Bar, Blum & Poe, Los Angeles
Summer Sculpture Show, CRG Gallery, New York

2011
The Air We Breathe, San Francisco Museum of Art, San Francisco
Wishing and Praying, CRG Gallery, New York

2009
Of Other Spaces, Bureau for Open Culture at Columbus College
of Art and Design, Columbus

2008
Sorry We're Closed, Galerie Rodolphe Janssen, Brussels
Duck Soup, La Mama, La Galleria, New York
The World Is All, Hudson Franklin Gallery, New York
Beyond A Memorable Fancy, Elizabeth Foundation for the Arts (EFA
Project Space), New York

Robert Beck

Born Towson, Maryland, in 1959
1993 Independent Study Program (Studio Program), Whitney
Museum of American Art, New York
1983 Undergraduate Film and Television, Tisch School of the Arts,
New York University, New York
Lived and worked in New York

Solo Exhibitions

2007
dust, Wexner Center for the Arts, Columbus
How am I to sign myself, CRG Gallery, New York

2006
Stephen Friedman Gallery, London
Olpalka Gallery, The Sage Colleges, Albany

2005
Anthony Meier Fine Arts, San Francisco

2004
CRG Gallery, New York
Art Basel Miami (The Design District), Miami

2003
Once Across the Mason-Dixon, Susan Inglett Gallery, New York

2002
Anthony Meier Fine Arts, San Francisco

2001
Drawings, CRG Gallery, New York

2000
Nature Mort, CRG Gallery, New York
Galerie Rainer Borgemeister, Berlin

1997
Susan Inglett Gallery, New York

1996
Susan Inglett Gallery, New York

2013
Love AIDS Riot Sex 1: Art AIDS Activism 1987-1995,
neue Gesellschaft für bildende Kunst e.V. (NGBK), Berlin

2012
À rebours, Adam Lindemann Gallery, New York
VHS, Museum of Art and Design, New York

2011
Politics is Personal, Stonescape, San Francisco
Crazy Lady, Schroeder Romero & Shredder, New York
Supply and Demand, Canzani Center Gallery, Columbus College of
Art & Design, Columbus
*Compass: Drawings of the Museum of Modern Art New York (The Judith
Rothschild Foundation Contemporary Drawings Collection)*, Berliner
Festspiele, Berlin
Wishing and Praying, CRG Gallery, New York
Looking at Music 3.0, The Museum of Modern Art, New York
Printer's Proof: A Decade of Fine Art Printing, Bertrand Delacroix
Gallery, New York

2010
Hunt & Chase, Salomon Contemporary, East Hampton, NY
Lush Life, Lehmann Maupin Gallery, New York
Robert Beck & Donald Moffet: Range, A collaborative work from 1997,
Marianne Boesky Gallery, New York
In and Out of Place, Zabludowicz Collection, London
The Language of Flowers, CRG Gallery, New York

2009
*Compass in Hand: Selections from The Judith Rothschild Foundation
Contemporary Drawings Collection*, The Museum of Modern Art, New York

2008
Looking Back: The 3rd White Columns Annual, White Columns, New York
Come In, We're Open!, Galerie Rodolphe Janssen, Brussels

2007
*Exhibitionism: An Exhibition of Exhibitions of Works from the Marieluise
Hessel Collection*, Center for , Center for Cultural Studies, Hessel
Museum of Art, Bard College, Annandale-on-Hudson, New York
On the Marriage Broker Joke, Office Baroque Gallery, Antwerp

2006
Twice Drawn, The Frances Young Tang Teaching Museum and Art
Gallery at Skidmore College, Saratoga Springs
The Last Time They Met, Stephen Friedman Gallery, London
Subject, Lyman Allyn Art Museum, New London, CT
Nightmares of Summer, Marvelli Gallery, New York
Armed: Contemporary Art and Violence, Mandeville Art Gallery, Union
College, Schnenectady, NY

2005
Past Presence: Childhood and Memory, Whitney Museum of American
Art, New York
Monuments for the USA, White Columns, New York; CCA Wattis
Institute for Contemporary Arts, San Francisco

Altered Spaces, Indianapolis Museum of Contemporary Art, Indianapolis
Heavenly, or A Slice of White, The Bertha and Karl Leubsdorf Art
Gallery, Hunter College, New York
Back from Nature: The Sportsman Redux, Institute of Contemporary
Art, Maine College of Art, Portland
10-Year Anniversary Show, Stephen Friedman Gallery, London

2004
Editions Fawbush: A Selection, Sandra Gering Gallery, New York
Needful Objects, The Cleveland Museum of Art, Ohio
Neo Queer, Center on Contemporary Art, Seattle
Your Heart Is No Match for My Love, The Soap Factory, Minneapolis

2003
Robert Beck, Russell Crotty, Siobhan Liddell, CRG Gallery, New York
Me, Myself and I, CRG Gallery, New York
*Somewhere Better Than This Place: Alternative Social Experience in the
Spaces of Contemporary Art*, Contemporary Arts Center, Cincinnati,
Little Triggers, Cohan Leslie and Browne, New York

2002
Different Class, Debs & Co., New York
Acquiring Tastes, Real Art Ways, Hartford
Arrested Development, Castle Gallery, The College of New Rochelle,
New Rochelle, New York

2001
The Draftman's Colors: 14 New Acquisitions, Whitney Museum of
American Arts, New York
Song Poems, Cohan Leslie and Browne, New York
Crossing the Line: Site Specific Works by Fifty Artists throughout Queens,
Queens Museum of Art, New York
In Cold Blood, Samuel Dorsky Museum of Art, State University of
New York at New Paltz, New York

2000
Wild Life, Reynolds Gallery, Richmond, VA
Destruction/Creation, Ubu Gallery, New York
Human/Nature, Caren Golden Fine Art, New York
Animal Magnetism, Bucknell Art Gallery, Bucknell University,
Lewisburg, PA

1999
Anni Albers, Robert Beck, Cadie Noland, Joan Semmel, and Nancy Shaver,
Matthew Marks Gallery, New York
Calender 2000, Center for Cultural Studies, Hessel Museum of Art,
Bard College, Annandale-on-Hudson, New York
Hindsight: Recent Work from the Permanent Collection, Whitney Museum
of American Art, New York

1998
Back-to-Back: Selected Fellows 1990-1998, New York Foundation for
the Arts, New York
Robert Beck and Jasmine Sian, Anthony Meier Fine Art, San Francisco
Images for the Millennium, Long Island Center of Photography, New York
Portraits: Inaugural Exhibition, Paul Morris Gallery, New York
Artists & Books: Picaron Editions 1997, Musée Matisse, Nice

1997
Investigations of New Photography and Film: The New God, Andrea
Rosen Gallery, New York
33rd Annual: Art on Paper, Weatherspoon Art Museum, Greensboro, NC
You Should Know Better / Truth and Artifice in Contemporary Photography,
Thread Waxing Space, New York

1996
Limited Edition Artists' Books since 1990, Brooke Alexander Gallery,
New York
What I Did On My Summer Vacation (benefit exhibition), White
Columns, New York
Sugar Mountain, White Columns, New York
Show and Tell, Lauren Wittels Gallery, New York

1995
Inaugural Exhibition, Morris-Healy Gallery, New York
Verisimilitude and the Utility of Doubt, White Columns, New York
Faggots: A Communiqué from North America, Centro Cultural Ricardo
Rojas, Universidad de Buenos Aires, Buenos Aires

1994
Violence / Business / Power, Neue Gesellschaft für bildende Kunst e.v., Berlin
Benefit Exhibition and Auction: Who Chooses Who, New Museum, New York

1992
7 Rooms, 7 Shows, P.S. 1 Contemporary Art Centre, New York
Gegendarstellung: Ethics and Aesthetics in Times of AIDS, Kunstverien,
Hamburg and Kunstmuseum, Lucerne

1991
Saint Vitas Dance, Suzanne Biederberg Gallery, Amsterdam
New Era Exhibition, New Era Building, New York
Queer, Butch, Femme…, Minor Injury Gallery, Brooklyn

1990
Greenberg Wilson Gallery, New York
AIDS / SIDA, Real Art Ways, Hartford, Connecticut
Looking at a Revolution, Simon Watson Project Space, New York

1989
Erotophobia, Simon Watson Project Space, New York
Group Material's AIDS Timeline, MATRIX, University Art Museum,
University of California at Berkeley, Berkeley Art Museum and
Pacific Film Archive

Library and Archives Canada Cataloguing in Publication

Robert Beck, Robert Buck : 2 March to 8 June 2013.

A catalogue of an exhibition of photography, drawing, mixed media and
    installation works by American artists Robert Beck and Robert Buck
    at Rennie Collection at Wing Sang held March 2 to June 8, 2013.
Contents: Introduction / Bob Rennie -- "How am I to sign myself?" on
    the art of Robert Buck / James Voorhies -- "Quel nom vais-je signer?
    : l'art de Robert Buck / James Voorhies -- Exhibited works --
    Collected works -- Select biography.
ISBN 978-0-9865961-6-2 (pbk.)

    1. Buck, Robert (Artist)--Exhibitions. I. Buck, Robert, artist.
Works. Selections. II. Voorhies, James Timothy. How am I to sign
myself?" on the art of Robert Buck. III. Rennie Collection, host
institution, issuing body

N6537.B82A4 2014   709.2   C2013-907988-2

ROBERT BECK

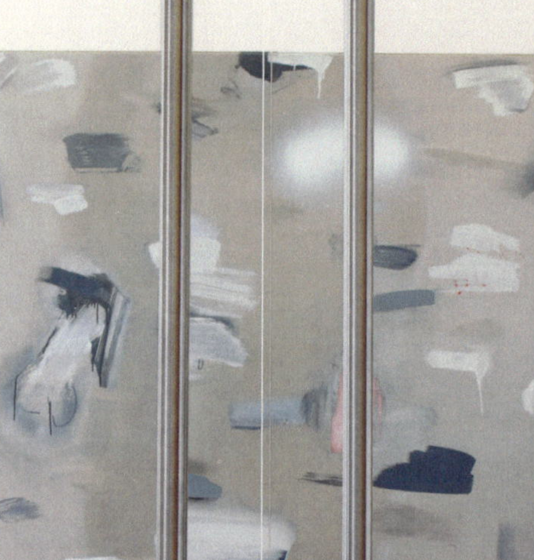

ROBERT BUCK

Published on the occasion of the exhibition Robert Beck /
Robert Buck at Rennie Collection at Wing Sang, Vancouver,
Canada, 2 March to 8 June 2013.

Text by James Voorhies
Editing by Wendy Chang
Copy editing by Cindy Richmond
Translation by André Roy
Design by Steedman Design
Photography by Blaine Campbell unless otherwise noted

Printed and bound by Artron Color Printing Co. Ltd., China
Publication © 2013 Rennie Collection
All artworks © Robert Beck / Robert Buck
Text © 2013 James Voorhies

www.renniecollection.org